To everyone who has been associated with FIRST TEACHER over the past eight years...every issue has been a celebration of teaching and learning.

And to the memory of Patrick Ginnane, one of our earliest contributors and supporters. He celebrated the relationship between the generations in a unique way.

CELEBRATE EVERY DAY

Hundreds of Celebrations for Early Childhood Classrooms

Edited by
Lisa Lyons Durkin

Art by
Debby Dixler

Projects by
Kathy Faggella

FIRST TEACHER PRESS
First Teacher, Inc./Bridgeport, CT

ISBN 0-9615005-5-7

Library of Congress Catalog Card Number 86-82829

Design by Alice Cooke, Alice Cooke Design Associates, NY

Cover Design by Alice Cooke; Illustration by Debby Dixler

Edited by Lisa Lyons Durkin

Associate Editor: Francesca DeMaria

Assistant Editor: Kathleen Hyson

Copy Editor: Martha A. Hayes

Manufactured in the United States of America.

Published by First Teacher Press, First Teacher, Inc.
P.O. Box 29, 60 Main Street, Bridgeport, CT 06602.

Distributed by: Gryphon House, Inc.
                  P.O. Box 275
                  Mt. Ranier, MD 20712

TABLE OF CONTENTS

TABLE OF CONTENTS

WE BELIEVE THAT

- life is full of celebrations and that we help children learn to celebrate both large and small occasions.
- children enjoy the spirit of a special occasion more in a secure, supportive, and relaxed atmosphere.
- children get the most out of celebrations if they can participate in the planning, decorating, food, and entertainment.
- celebrations are a wonderful break in classroom routines and through them, children develop important thinking skills and concepts.
- children learn about other countries and cultures through celebrations.
- each child deserves one celebration in her honor—besides her birthday—each year.
- childcare programs should focus on the daily celebrations—friendship, small accomplishments, changes in nature, and just being alive.

CELEBRATIONS— BIG AND SMALL

SHERRY BURRELL

As caregivers, we can help children learn how to celebrate both the large and the small things in life. Celebrations should convey simple messages to young children. Life is full of opportunities to praise accomplishments and show appreciation.

When planning for these celebrations, we most often think of the "big" celebrations: the holidays, birthday parties, and the special events. But, there are also smaller events to celebrate with children: learning to tie a shoe, putting on a jacket all alone for the first time, or learning to take turns with the tricycle.

Some children have a hard time dealing with celebrations that might upset the normal routine, might overexcite them, or might even put them in the spotlight when they are not ready for it. It is our job to help children enjoy the spirit of the occasion in a secure, supportive, and relaxed atmosphere.

THE "BIG" CELEBRATIONS

Sometimes, children are overstimulated weeks, even months, ahead of a holiday by the TV ads, newspaper ads, and store displays that surround them. There are some things we can do in school to balance the experience for them.

■ Keep to the regular schedule—mealtimes, nap, playtime—as much as possible to make the children feel secure.

■ Provide lots of opportunities, like circletime, stories, and table activities, for children to discuss their feelings about the upcoming event. You can ask questions like these to draw out their feelings:

• "How do you celebrate Thanksgiving at your house?"

• "What makes you feel happiest about this holiday?"

• "Is there anything about the holiday that makes you feel sad or afraid?"

■ Provide a few simple holiday-related activities—making decorations or handmade gifts—close to the time of the holiday. Be sure to provide a variety of materials and encourage each child to feel that whatever he makes is worthwhile.

■ If an inschool celebration is planned, avoid holding it first thing in the morning, just before naptime, or just before going home. Allow time for you and the children to both prepare for and recover from the experience. Mid-morning perhaps? Remember that a two-year-old group will probably enjoy no more than 30 minutes of special activity. Plan the rest of the day as normally as possible.

■ While inviting all children to join in, offer a more calming alternative for those children who are not feeling comfortable joining in the celebration—table toys, books, crayons.

THE "SMALL" CELEBRATIONS

Daily, there are a number of things we can consider doing with children to help them feel good about themselves, while helping them learn how to celebrate the small things in life.

■ Hand a child a smiling paper face, send him a "cele-gram" (a short note of encouragement), or spend some "special" one-to-one time with him to celebrate his small accomplishments or new skills. For example: "You've worked hard today." "You zipped up your jacket all by yourself!"

■ Encourage each child to think of something nice to say or do for someone else—the custodian, a student teacher, the cook, a parent or relative. Help the child to write a special note of thanks to someone. (The child dictates and illustrates.) For example: "Dear Ms. Cook, I liked your spaghetti today. It tasted good in my tummy."

■ Celebrate any and all of the "small" things you and your children enjoy in everyday life:

• First snow
• A rainy day
• First buds, green leaves, grass
• First tadpoles in the pond
• Classroom pet having babies
• Longest/shortest day of the year
• First orange leaf of fall
• New books for the library

Once you get started, you and the children will come up with lots of your own ideas.

When our childcare programs focus on the daily celebrations of friendship, small accomplishments, and just being alive, children begin to learn that is perhaps the simple messages in life that are most important in all celebrations—even the "big" ones.

PARTY GIVER'S GUIDE

JANET HOROWITZ

Party celebrations for holidays, birthdays, and special events are happy times for sharing fun, learning, escitement, and joy—a time for feeling good! But unfortunately, teachers often report that they feel tense and pressured from planning and managing parties—and with good reason since they tend to do all the work themselves.

Here are some suggestions, which do not guarantee a successful party, but do give you a way to share the preparation and fun of the party with your children.

■ Involve the children from the very beginning.
■ Keep the celebration simple.
■ Use a checklist for planning.

Circletime is a good place to begin involving your children. Over a period of days, talk together about the reason for the party and about decorations, entertainment, and food.

You will probably want to talk with some of the children on their own—those children who will need special encouragement to join in.

Planning the entertainment—games and music—can be entertaining in itself. Invite the children to share and show each other and you what they think will be fun.

With the children, choose foods that are simple, but enjoyed by everyone. Some treats can be made by children a day or two before the party—cakes and cookies; others, like popcorn, can be made at the party.

Making decorations can begin days before the party or simply be done by a few children just before the party starts.

Keeping the party simple cuts down on planning time and cleanup. A simple party is no less exciting or fun for the children. It is usually more fun for all because everyone has played a part from the very beginning, so everyone is enjoying the actual food, decorations, and entertainment they planned and made.

A lovely way to thank everyone for their help—parents included—is to put an appreciation chart on the wall, "Thank you, Jodi, for handing out the napkins. Thanks to Jim and his dad for baking the cupcakes." You and the children can construct it the day after the party at circletime. The chart also reminds everyone of the wonderful time they had and gives children practice in recall skills.

STEP-BY-STEP PLANNING GUIDE

Before the Party

1. Two-four weeks:
■ Decide what kind of party you will have and who will help—children, parents, others in community.

2. Two weeks:
■ Have children make the invitations (artwork) on which you can paste a copy of your written invitation.
■ Plan the menu.
■ Plan the decorations.

3. One week:
■ Shop with the children for food staples and decoration materials.

4. Three days:
■ Clean up room with the children.
■ Start to make decorations.

5. Two days:
■ Finish decorations and hang them up.

6. One day:
■ Put together everything you will need.
■ Set up tables and put decorations on them.
■ Prepare any food that can be made in advance.

The Big Day

■ Prepare last minute food early with the children—punch, sandwiches.
■ ENJOY!!!

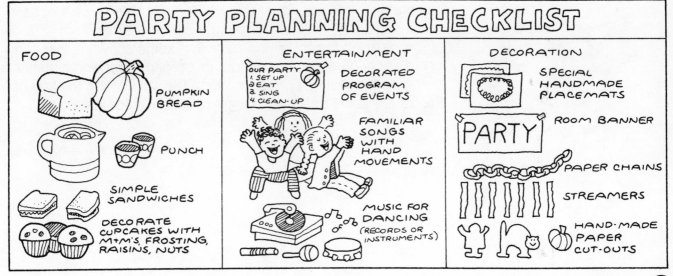

PARTY PLANNING CHECKLIST

FOOD
PUMPKIN BREAD
PUNCH
SIMPLE SANDWICHES
DECORATE CUPCAKES WITH M+M'S, FROSTING, RAISINS, NUTS

ENTERTAINMENT
OUR PARTY 1. SET UP 2. EAT 3. SING 4. CLEAN-UP
DECORATED PROGRAM OF EVENTS
FAMILIAR SONGS WITH HAND MOVEMENTS
MUSIC FOR DANCING (RECORDS OR INSTRUMENTS)

DECORATION
SPECIAL HANDMADE PLACEMATS
PARTY ROOM BANNER
PAPER CHAINS
STREAMERS
HAND-MADE PAPER CUT-OUTS

PARTY SKILLS

MARTHA A. HAYES

Remember the fun you have had over the years planning and participating in parties—for your friends, family, dolls, and stuffed animals? Many of the important thinking skills you use today were developed during those early parties. Are you providing opportunities for the children in your class to learn through giving parties?

Most children enjoy parties; you can use their natural enthusiasm to good advantage when showing them how or letting them experiment with planning different types of celebrations. Besides all the skills, they will be learning how to make other people happy. While working on all aspects of a party, children will be practicing skills they will need later in school and life.

Examine your housekeeping area to see what additional props you might add to inspire some dramatic play on the theme of partygiving. Here are some suggestions:
• Flatware
• Toy birthday cakes
• Calendars
• Placemats
• Mailboxes for invitations
• Tea sets
• Empty food cartons

Give children some suggestions for dramatic play on a rainy day. For example, ask what would happen if the three bears invited Goldilocks to their house for a party. What kind of food would they serve? How would the bears entertain Goldilocks? Would she steal in and try out their food and furniture before the party? Or, what kind of party might the three little pigs have to celebrate their victory over the wolf? Might they have a house rebuilding party—could this be in the block corner?

The chart on the following page lists some activities that can occur as children are thinking out or preparing for and actually taking part in real or pretend parties. The skills along the top of the list are some of those thought to be basic for learning.

	Recalling Details	Sequence	Following Directions	Predicting	Cause and Effect	Comparing	Classifying	Main Idea	Drawing Conclusions	Generalizing	Picture Interpretation	Realism or Fantasy
1. Decide to have a party.								X	X			
a. Talk about favorite ones.	X					X	X					
b. Talk about special times that can be celebrated.										X		
2. Decide what kind of party to have.				X			X	X				
3. Decide what to do to get ready for party.		X										
a. Make lists.		X	X									
b. Plan schedule.		X	X									
4. Decide who to invite.									X			
5. Write and/or decorate the invitations.			X									
6. Choose menu.							X					
a. Recall favorite foods.	X											
b. Pick out certain foods for special days.							X					
7. Shop for food.							X					
8. Decorate room and/or table.			X									
a. Pick or make flowers.			X									
b. Make placemats.			X								X	
c. Choose dishes.							X					
9. Prepare food.		X										
10. Set table.		X	X									
11. Entertain guests.			X									
a. Choose games.							X					
b. Tell favorite stories.	X											X
c. Put on plays or puppet shows.			X									X

HOW TO USE THIS BOOK

KATHY FAGGELLA

Holidays and parties are an exciting way to teach young children—skills, concepts, all about ourselves and people of different cultures.

All too often, unfortunately, celebrations become a headache for teachers. They take up so much time and energy that they are no longer enjoyable.

Also, it is possible for the celebrations, themselves, to become routine. When I was in second grade, I knew we could look forward to having pretzels and grape drink every time there was a holiday.

Celebrate Every Day shows you how to avoid both party pitfalls— the headaches and the routines. There are suggestions for all the major holidays and, we think, all the possible reasons you might have for "throwing a party" in your classroom.

This book is an anthology of all the best ideas from our FIRST TEACHER writers over the years, so every activity, project, recipe, and song is classroom tested and child approved. You will find that some of the articles are very personal—the writers are sharing their joy and sense of excitement.

No one could expect you to fit every celebration in this book into your curriculum, nor does every one you do choose have to be followed to the letter. You are the only one who knows your special group and its needs. The age of the children you work with and the size of the group will determine the complexity of the special occasion.

During a holiday celebration, be sure to include the legend that accompanies the holiday. For young children, this can be the most enjoyable and often the most memorable part of the festivities. Sometimes, the reason for a holiday can become lost in its celebration.

It is possible to learn about a holiday in your local library or from friends, relatives, or parents. The celebration of a holiday from a culture other than our own can provide a wonderful way for foreign-born parents to contribute to the class. In fact, it is often best to choose the holidays you will celebrate by the ethnic composition of your group of children.

Remember that celebrations are important learning experiences for your children. Even at a tea party for dolls, a child gets practice in classification, one-to-one correspondence, creative thinking, and social skills.

Use the celebrations in this book any time you need a lift. It's hard to celebrate Christmas in May, but Chinese New Year works well during any cold, miserable stretch of winter. Sometimes, spontaneous celebrations—when everyone seems down in the dumps—can be the best kind.

HOLIDAYS

INTRODUCING— HOLIDAYS

NANCY MCKEEVER

Holidays always involve many feelings, much excitement, anticipation, and sometimes fear—especially for young children who often don't know what to expect. Teachers can provide a relaxed atmosphere where adults and children can take part in the celebration at their own pace.

We can help the children we teach deal with their fears and expectations about the holidays. Because three-, four-, and five-year-olds have little sense of time, they may need careful explanations to understand, for instance, that Halloween will be in three days. Counting the days may satisfy some; however, others must be told, "You'll go to bed, get up, come to school, go home, go to bed, and then, it will be Halloween." This may sound repetitious to an adult, but it can really help a child understand the time sequence.

Often, we can avoid the whole subject with a child under three; but three-, four-, and five-year-olds seem to have a sense that important occasions are approaching. Helping them begin to have a sense of time is part of helping them deal with their anticipation.

Children love to help with the preparations for a holiday. One child I know deals with his anticipation of Christmas by making decorations for all the windows in his house. Each day before the holiday, he gets out paper, markers, scissors, and begins. Sometimes, he does one window pane, other times, ten. It doesn't really matter if all the windows are done in time for the big day, This is his own very special way of dealing with a holiday planned mainly by adults.

So, let your children do a little something each day before the holiday, beginning when you sense their need for an outlet. Let them work through some of their excitement—and sometimes, fear—and learn more about the holiday at the same time.

This chapter is chock full of ideas—projects, games, songs, even field trips—to make the waiting easy and fun and each holiday, itself, a true learning adventure!

CHRISTMAS THANKSGIVING HALLOWEEN BIRTHDAY

18

DECORATE COLUMBUS DAY

JOANNE BELL

Parties are always fun. All of the games, songs, and activities let children have a good time. They also help children practice social skills in meaningful situations.

Decorations add atmosphere to a party and make it more exciting. Just as decorating your centers and classrooms motivates young children to learn, party decorations can put everyone into a festive spirit. If the children can make these themselves, it's best of all, because the fun and learning is extended beyond the party.

The following are some ideas and examples of simple childmade decorations using Columbus Day as the main theme. However, these ideas can be adapted to fit any holiday or season.

Tablecloth

Use tissue paper, crepe paper, or large wrapping paper. Let children cover the tablecloth with stickers or crayon drawings. You could duplicate little pictures with a Columbus Day theme, since stickers might not be available. The children then could color, cut, and paste these on the tablecloth. For variety, use construction paper or cut up the tissue paper into placemats and let children decorate them.

Another festive tablecloth can be made by using blue crepe paper streamers to drape around the side of an old sheet. Then, let children cut out pictures of ships and glue them on the cloth above the drape.

Napkin Rings

Use cardboard rolls cut to two inches. Wrap tissue paper around each and decorate with stickers or cutout pictures.

Garlands

Children can make paper boats, telescopes, and flags, and attach them to string or crepe paper streamers. These could be used as large garlands to hang on doors, windows, or tables, or from ceilings.

Centerpieces

Have children fold small pieces of colored cardboard in half to form a stand. Paste on children's drawings or bulletin board decorations.

You could also use some of the three-dimensional artwork of the children as a centerpiece. For Columbus Day, take a styrofoam meat tray and glue crumpled blue cellophane or other blue paper inside. Let each child make small boats out of walnut shells or egg carton sections, toothpicks, and paper sails.

Other ideas for party centerpieces include puppets propped up on cardboard rolls; found materials such as leaves, pinecones; and houses made of milk cartons.

Mobiles

These can be fun to make and take the place of a centerpiece, if your table will be too loaded with goodies. Hang one over each table. You make big ships as the base; then, let each child make a sail to hang on.

Mural

A final idea could be a wall of artwork. This would make the perfect backdrop for songs like "Blow the Man Down," "Merrily We Roll Along," or "Row, Row, Row, Your Boat," or stories. To get started, read "The Three Ships" by Lilian Allard or another poem found in *The Poetry Place Anthology* by Instructor Books. "Christopher Columbus" by Stephen Vincent Benet might appeal to the children. The children could illustrate the poems or draw what they remember—this also develops comprehension and listening skills.

Whichever decorations you choose, have a good time at the party and by all means, let the children "do it themselves."

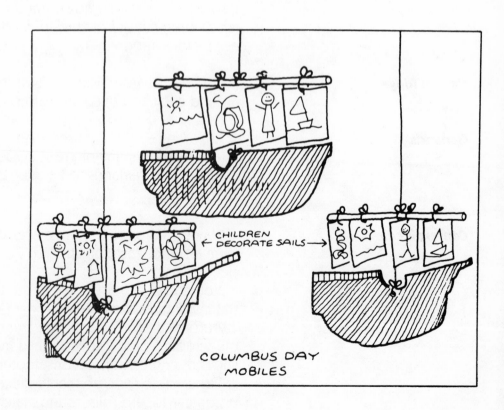

← CHILDREN DECORATE SAILS →

COLUMBUS DAY MOBILES

HARVEST SUKKAH

MARY ANN HALL

We all need to be more aware of the origins of the food used during our daily meals. There are many beautiful ways to express appreciation for the fruits and vegetables of the harvest that often end up on our tables. One of the most festive ways to celebrate the harvest is to observe and participate in some of the traditions of Sukkot, the Autumn Festival of Jewish People. It is a celebration of thanksgiving that includes building a harvest hut, the Sukkah. You might want to introduce this idea through the Hebrew song below.

The words say:
The Sukkah, how beautiful.
How good it is to sit in the Sukkah.

BUILD A SUKKAH

There are many ways to do this. We found that a very successful and relatively easy way was to start with a large refrigerator box. We cut out the top and a small door on one of the sides. We painted the box, and then, we gathered branches to lay across the top. We made a list of fruits and vegetables that would last a while without being refrigerated. Our list included: oranges, lemons, squash, pumpkins, gourds, tomatoes, carrots, parsnips, apples, onions, garlic, peppers, and eggplant.

As the children brought in their foods from home, I threaded the fruits and vegetables, with a big needle and heavy thread, so that we could hang them from the branches resting on top of the Sukkah. We put the heavier, harder foods on the roof.

Our harvest house became a favorite spot to visit, especially when a child needed a quiet, alone time.

I left surprises in the hut—sometimes, books; sometimes, paper and writing materials; and sometimes, a cassette recorder with several tapes. You'll think of other things. The children were thrilled with this whole idea and I must confess, so was I.

HALLOWEEN PARTY

DR. MARGERY A. KRANYIK

Parents and teachers are becoming increasingly concerned about the safety of young children trick-or-treating in a neighborhood on Halloween night. Since the costumes and goodies are important to youngsters, as they are the focus of any Halloween celebration, consider organizing a trick-or-treat party at school, involving the parents.

You may be able to eliminate the door-to-door activity if you open your classroom to a Halloween party. Invitations may be sent or given out. Your inschool celebration still can include costumes, treats, and games, and also be well supervised.

Invite your young guests and their parents with instructions to appear in costume with a trick-or-treat sack. To carry on the Halloween tradition, ask each parent to have a treat available for each young guest.

Consider some of the following activities for the party games. They are easy to prepare from inexpensive materials.

Scary Sounds

Tape record some "scary" sounds to be used as background sound effects. Sounds, such as rattling chains, a meowing cat, footsteps, creaking doors, and moans and groans, can provide excitement and laughter without being frightening. The children can make their scariest sounds on the tape, also.

Halloween Mural

Cover a wall with large sheets of drawing paper or cut-up supermarket bags. Give out some crayons and have children draw their own Halloween picture. Give prizes for the scariest, most special, or funniest.

Goblin Game

Ask everyone to form a circle and play the following game. The words are sung to the tune of the familiar "Farmer in the Dell," and the game is played similarly. "The goblin in the dark, the goblin in the dark, Heigh-Ho, it's Halloween, the goblin in the dark." One child starts in the center of a circle as the "goblin." As the children march around, the goblin takes a ghost in the next verse, a cat in the following verse, and so on, until the circle is filled with such creepy creatures as a goblin, ghost, cat, spook, pumpkin, witch—anything suggestive of Halloween.

Long Faces

From a large supermarket bag, cut an oval long enough to go from the children's heads to knees and wide enough to cover their bodies. Have them draw features with crayons or felt-tipped pens. Let everyone hold up their faces and march around in a parade, using your taped scary sounds as background music.

Ten Little Pumpkins

Have the children cut pumpkins—ghosts, witches, black cats—from construction paper. Sing the song to the tune of "Ten Little Indians." "One little, two little, three little pumpkins. Four little, five little, six little pumpkins. Seven little, eight little, nine little pumpkins. Ten pumpkins on the fence." The witches can be "flying in the sky"; cats can be "in a tree"; and ghosts "in the air."

Haunted House

Use a large appliance carton. Turn it so the open end is at the bottom. Have children decorate the outside with appropiate Halloween figures. Cut a door in the front and one in the rear. On the inside of the carton, tie a piece of string across the top. Attach pieces of yarn to the string, so they hang down and tickle your goblins as they walk through the haunted house. Use your tape of scary sounds as background.

Have an instant developing camera available to take each child's picture before he leaves. This will serve as a reminder of a good time and a new way to celebrate Halloween.

SKELETON
STICK WHITE ADHESIVE TAPE TO BLACK SHIRT AND SLACKS COVER HEAD WITH BLACK FELT

PRINCESS
WEAR A LON DRESS AND A HAT MADE WITH A CONE OF PAPER AN A SCARF OU OF THE TOP

PRINCE
MAKE AN ALUMINUM FOIL COVERED CARDBOARD SWORD. WEAR BOOTS AND A BELT BUCKLED OVER A LONG SHIRT

SCARECROW
WEAR OLD CLOTHES AND STUFF HAY INTO CUFFS ON SLEEVES TIE AT WRISTS AND ANKLES WITH YARN FOR HEAD. CRUMPLE UP A BROWN GROCERY BAG OPEN UP AND CUT OUT EYES, NOSE, AND A MOUTH GLUE ON HAT HAIR PLACE OVER HEAD AND TIE LOOSELY AROUND NECK WITH YARN

BUNCH OF GRAPES
PURCHASE PURPLE BALLOONS TIE EACH TO A STRING AND TIE TO CHILD'S BODY CUT OUT A PAPER LEAF AND VINE TO WEAR ON HEAD.

BOX IDEAS
USE EMPTY CARD-BOARD BOXES TO MAKE A
- ROBOT
- T V SET
- BOX OF CEREAL
- PLAYING CARD

TRICK OR TREAT BAG

YOU'LL NEED:

 scissors

 stapler

 grocery bag

 crayons or felt tip markers

 reflective tape

 12"x2" strip of cardboard

WHAT TO DO:

Cut bag shape from grocery bag.

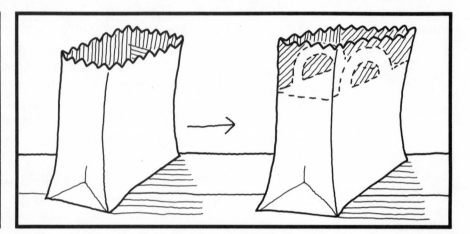

Staple both handles together. Reinforce with a strip of cardboard folded and stapled to center of the 2 handles.

cardboard strip

Draw Jack O' Lanterns, cats, and other designs on bag. If possible, stick on reflective tape.

IN THE PUMPKIN PATCH

MARTHA SAYRE

The Thanksgiving season is a good time to do pumpkin activities. The native Americans sowed pumpkin seeds in their cornfields and shared the idea with the pilgrims. A golden pumpkin pie, flavorful with spices, is traditional in most American homes on Thanksgiving Day. You and your children can use this colorful fruit in creative ways.

Pumpkin Cooking

Pumpkin butter is a good, spicy treat for cooking with young children.

For Pumpkin Butter, *you'll need:*

- 2 cups cooked pumpkin
- 1 cup molasses
- 1 teaspoon cinnamon
- ½ teaspoon nutmeg
- ½ teaspoon ginger
- ¼ teaspoon cloves

Cook all ingredients well, stirring all the time, until thick and buttery.

Pumpkin Prints

Cut pieces of pumpkin into various shapes and sizes—or cut a design into the smooth outer surface of the pieces.

Make a paint pad for each color to be used. For each paint pad, fold a wet cloth or paper towel and place it in a shallow dish. Sprinkle it with powdered paint or brush on tempera paint. A little water can be added, if the paint pad dries. Let the children press a cut pumpkin piece into a paint pad and then down on paper to make one or more prints.

Printing is a fascinating activity for children because it pleases them to repeat their own designs. Pumpkin prints can be used for holiday wrapping paper, gift tags, or greeting cards.

Pumpkin Patch

With the children, fill small grocery sacks with wads of crumpled newspapers. Tie with green yarn to form stems. Then, let children paint sacks with orange tempera paint. When dry, create a pumpkin patch in one corner of the room. Make vines with green yarn and tie sack pumpkins onto them. Add leaves cut from green construction paper.

As the orange pumpkins peek out of the green leaves, play "Way Down Yonder in the Pumpkin Patch," using the "Paw Paw Patch" tune.

Pumpkin Carpentry

Let children hammer nails into a pumpkin. The tough rind is a good medium for a successful experience, when first learning to use a hammer.

Pumpkin Math

Paste dried seeds on cards. Use for counting, learning sets, and matching games.

PREPARE A FEAST

SANDRA GRATIAS

Holiday time usually means lots of food preparation. Children can help and there are many things they can learn from cooking. Involving children will take longer, but it helps them make the wait for a special occasion easier and it can be fun for all. Plan a Thanksgiving feast at school and invite parents, another class, or perhaps the residents of a local senior citizens' home to share the bounty.

The first step is planning the menu and the children should be included. Tell them what you have planned already (such as turkey with stuffing) and let them choose some things to go with it. Explain about the food groups and let them make simple choices— "We need a green vegetable. Should we have peas or beans?" Help them learn to take the needs of others into account.

Let's say you come up with this menu: turkey with stuffing, mashed potatoes, gravy, peas, carrots, stuffed celery, homemade rolls, and pumpkin pie. Next, you must shop. Bring the children along. (Perhaps, you will have to make a few trips, each time with a small group.) Give each child a label or magazine picture to match up with labels in the store. Point out how things are grouped—carrots with fresh vegetable, flour with baking items. Let children hand things from the cart to you as you name them at the checkout counter. Identify the coins you use. Let everyone carry something back to school.

The biggest part of the project is the food preparation. Give yourselves plenty of time. Make what you can ahead of time. In the menu above, the pie, rolls, and stuffed celery can be prepared the day before. Make sure you have everything assembled before you begin, so you won't have to leave your young "assistants" alone while you fetch something.

Preparing the menu provides lots of small motor practice: tearing bread for stuffing, peeling carrots, using a handbeater, breaking eggs, sifting, scrubbing potatoes, kneading and shaping rolls, rolling pie dough, stuffing celery, measuring, and pouring. Put a rubber band around the measuring cup to mark the level you need. As you all work, describe the feel of the ingredients, the smells, and the colors. Count and describe quantity and size and talk about cooking time to introduce math concepts. Let children compare raw and cooked potatoes and pie dough. (Heat causes physical change. That's science.) Read the recipes aloud to show the practical use of reading and following directions. Offer instructions, assistance, and encouragement, but don't be a perfectionist.

On the big day, let children help set the table (counting and one-to-one correspondence), and help serve. Tell everyone that they helped. They will be very proud, and so will you.

INDIAN PUDDING

YOU'LL NEED:

 1/4 cup storebought cornmeal

 2 stones for grinding

 2 eggs

 1 package frozen corn nibblets

 3/4 cup molasses

 1 tsp. salt (or less)

 1 tsp cinnamon

 1/2 tsp ginger

 1 cup cold milk

 2 Tblsp. butter

 4 cups hot milk

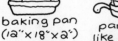 baking pan (12"x 18"x 2")

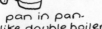 pan in pan - like double boiler

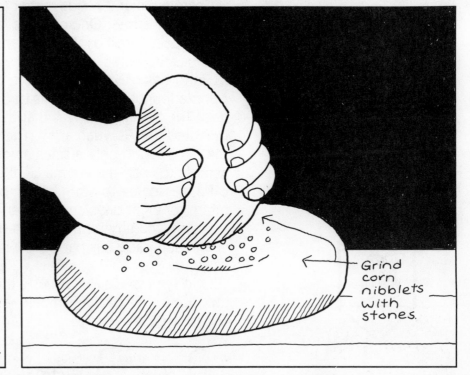

Grind corn nibblets with stones.

WHAT TO DO:

1.
Make your own GROUND CORNMEAL. Use 2 stones to grind it. 1 stone should be flat with a hollow in the middle, the other should be rounded and heavy.

2.
Then, place a package of frozen corn nibblets in the oven on a cookie sheet. Dry out in a low (150°-200°F) oven. When hard and dry, grind to meal.

3.
Slowly, stir 1/4 cup homemade cornmeal and 1/4 cup storebought cornmeal into hot milk. Milk should be in a pan over another pan of boiling water (like a double boiler).

4.
Cook hot milk and cornmeal for 20 minutes.

5.
Add the rest of the ingredients (except the cold milk) to the cornmeal mixture.

6.
Pour mixture into a 12"x 18"x 2" pan. Pour 1 cup cold milk over it. DO NOT MIX. Bake at 325°F for 50 minutes. Serve warm.

HANUKKAH

HARRIET ETTENSON

There are many holidays that fall in December about the same time as Christmas. One of these is Hanukkah or the Festival of the Lights, celebrated by Jewish people. This holiday celebrates two miracles.

Hundreds of years before the birth of Christ, the Jewish people fought the Assyrians to defend their right to worship one god. The first miracle was that the small band of Jewish soldiers defeated the Assyrian army. The second miracle happened when the Jews found only a small amount of holy oil left in their Temple to keep the Eternal Light burning. They immediately sent off a messenger to bring back more oil. The messenger did not return for eight days and to everyone's amazement, at the end of that time, the tiny bit of oil was still burning. They proclaimed, "A great miracle has happened here," and made a festival in celebration.

One symbol for Hanukkah is the dreidel, a four-sided, square top, used in a special game. It has a Hebrew letter on each side. The letters look like this:

They stand for the saying "Nes Gadol Hayah Sham" which means *A Great Miracle Happened There*. Everyone, in this game of chance, starts with 10-15 items, which are traditionally pennies, raisins, or nuts. Each player puts one into the pot or the middle of the circle where they are sitting. Each player takes a turn to spin the dreidel. Whether he wins or loses depends on which letter turns up. Each letter also stands for a Yiddish word. *Nun* means "nisht" or "nothing" and the player who gets that letter takes nothing. *Gimmel* means "gantz" or "all" and the player takes everything in the pot. *Hay* means "halb" or "half" and the player takes half. *Shin* means "shtel" or "put in" and the player adds items to the pot. A dreidel can be purchased at the local novelty store for under 50 cents or you can make one out of self-hardening clay.

To recall the two miracles, every Hanukkah Jews light a Menorah, a candleholder for eight candles and a candle that sits above the others and is used to light them. The Menorah is lit each night for eight nights. This ceremony is accompanied by special Hanukkah prayers. On the first night, one candle is lit; on the second night, two; and so on until the last night, when all eight candles are lit. Each night the Menorah is lit, each child in the family receives a present in celebration of the Festival of Lights.

DREIDEL-SHAPED MENORAH

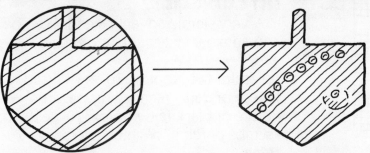

YOU'LL NEED:

self-hardening clay

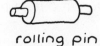
rolling pin

plastic knife

birthday candles

WHAT TO DO:

1.
Roll out self-hardening clay like a pancake and pound it down to about ½" thickness.

2.
Cut out dreidel shape with plastic knife.

3.
Push in 8 little holes with a birthday candle.

4.
With some extra clay, make a mound for the SHAMMUS, the ninth candle that sits above the others.

5.
Push in a little hole in the mound for the SHAMMUS.

6.
Stick a birthday candle in each hole.

ADVENT CALENDARS

KATHY FAGGELLA

Advent calendars help young children deal with the anticipation of the holiday season and they also help them develop their sense of time.

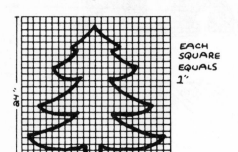

EACH SQUARE EQUALS 1"

24"

24"

FELT CALENDARS

A very simple advent calendar can be made with felt. Children add an ornament to the tree each day before Christmas.

You'll Need:
• piece of felt, approx. 36" x 24" (red, white)
• piece of dark green felt, approx. 24" x 24"
• piece of black felt, approx. 10" x 12" or fabric marker
• scraps of felt in brighter colors

What to Do:
1. Glue the red or white felt to a 36" x 24" side and slip in a dowel. Tie with yarn and hang.
2. Using the guide at the left, cut out a Christmas tree shape from green felt.
3. Glue the green tree onto the red or white background. Place it near the top.
4. Use the black felt to cut out numbers 1-25. Glue the numbers in calendar form under the tree. (Optional: Instead of cutout numbers, use a fabric marker and write them in.)
5. With children, cut out simple ornament shapes from scraps. You will need 25.
6. Let children place one ornament next to each number. Each day, place one on the tree. Save the star for last!

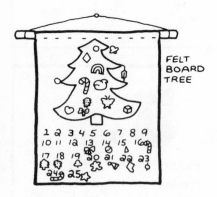

FELT BOARD TREE

STICKER ADVENT TREES

To make simple, individualized advent reminders, cut tree shapes from green construction paper and add tiny stickers or gummed stars each day until the holiday. The tree, then, can become an ornament to hang.

A STICKER ADVENT TREE

GUMMED STARS →

CELEBRATE THE SEASON

JEANNINE PEREZ

This year, you and your children can help each other celebrate the holidays with childlike wonder and anticipation. In my classroom at the Fairchild Daycare Center, we emphasize the joys of giving, the fun and excitement of receiving, and we use all five senses to get the most from each hour and day. The holidays are, and always have been, reflections of whatever we bring to them.

THE JOY OF GIVING

Starting early in the fall, and picking up speed after Thanksgiving, we make the most of the natural generosity of children. We try to do as many "giving" projects as time allows— gifts for parents, for our "adopted" grandparents in a nearby nursing home, gifts for friends, and even gifts for the Center itself. Here are a few ideas to spur your own creativity.

■ In the fall, we had our own "garage sale," and the children sent the money to Africa for food. It wasn't a great amount, but the involvement and interest on the part of the children was fantastic!

■ I read *The Giving Tree*, by Shel Silverstein to the children. Last year, we drew sequential pictures to illustrate the story and made a bulletin board of them. The story will bring out many ideas and discussions and makes a perfect beginning for the season of giving.

■ We used the rind of oranges, making the peel as long a strip as possible, gathered them into a cheesecloth square (5") with a few whole cloves and sticks of cinnamon. These are kitchen spice bags, activated by boiling in a little water, when desired.

■ We made our own gift wrap with shelf paper or newsprint that the children had stamped with cut vegetables and tempera paint. We used the tops of carrots, green pepper halves, and potatoes in which designs had been carved as our stampers.

■ We made new clothes for the dolls in the Center, and did some repair on stuffed toys. This was so much fun that we went further and refurbished the dollhouse with homemade furniture as our gift to the Center.

■ Milk cartons—individual ones—were saved, washed out, cut down, and painted silver. Then, we started slips of plants; I let each child decorate his own with tinsel, glitter and ribbon, and by Christmas, they were sturdy and beautiful plants.

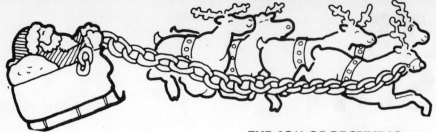

THE JOY OF RECEIVING

We also share the wide-eyed excitement of anticipation of WHAT might be in packages and stockings meant for us!

■ A fun game for circletime starts with a festively wrapped package, with a hinged opening on one side. We try to guess which of the Center's toys is in the box, with the aid of clues. ("It's soft and blue and as big as a loaf of bread.") When guessed, we let the child who guessed correctly hide another item and provide clues.

■ Another game using the box might be to put 10 to 12 items on a tray. The children close their eyes and the leader puts one item in the box. Then, the children try to say what is missing. The child, who remembers correctly is the next leader. With younger children, use less items.

■ In Art, I help the children draw big boxes on newsprint and they draw WHAT IS IN THE BOX. If they dictate to me, I'll write their ideas on the drawing.

■ In Language Arts, I use experience charts to record class discussions on the most special gift they remember. One year, we arranged this into a class poem, illustrated it, and hung it on the door.

■ We also made up a fun list of famous people and what their favorite gift would be. (Snoopy, Dr. Seuss, President Reagan) The discussion was interesting and stretched their thinking.

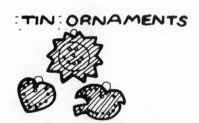

DECORATIONS

We decorated the Center in many ways to put everyone in the holiday mood.

■ We made the bulletin board into a huge window with curtains and used it as a frame for children's art, showing what was seen by peeking through.

■ Collages of gifts, holiday decorations, or winter scenes are always favorites. These can be individual or group efforts.

■ Our center received an old wire display rack that we used in the bathroom in the winter to dry mittens on. At Christmas time one year (and ever after), we decorated it with handmade ornaments, making one apiece each day. They included paper chains, ornaments from salt clay that were painted and glittered, pipe cleaner candy canes, god's eyes made from sticks and yarn, string dipped in glue and glitter and set in strange shapes to dry on waxed paper, wreaths made from plastic can lids with centers removed and wrapped with yarn. Each ornament was labeled with the child's name and the date, and each child took home a sack of ornaments for their own tree on the last day before vacation.

CELEBRATE THE SENSES

What is the recipe for holiday magic? It is a time to use all your senses! Experience the tastes and smells of cinnamon, orange, and pine. See the bright brave reds and greens against new snow or barren brown landscapes, the shimmer of silver, and sparkle of white snow. Hear the sound of bells and carols. Feel the slippery chill of ice, prickly needles, and softness of velvet. Help children experience using ALL their senses. Here are some special things to do.

■ Make experience charts—some written together in circletime, others in small groups, or one to one. Children can illustrate later. Examples: The cold wind makes me feel _____ . Snowflakes look like _____ . The smell I like best at holiday time is

_____ .

■ Play Christmas records; ask children to sit very still and listen to sounds they hear. Have them draw pictures on a large sheet of newsprint as they listen.

■ Read or tell stories by candlelight. (Keep candles far away from little hands.) Draw the curtains and use candles with holiday scents.

■ Take a winter walk. Ask questions. Is it different than summer? What are the main colors? What do you see? Hear? Can you see your breath? Where are the animals? What birds do you see? Are there any insects on the ground? Where are the butterflies?

■ Ring bells with different tones. Talk about the sounds they make and ask questions to stimulate creative thinking. Which might be used by Santa? In church? Put the bells on the science table for children to ring. At circletime, have children close their eyes. Ring a bell, and let children decide which one you rang.

■ Rewrite "The Twelve Days of Christmas," after first singing the original. (Children may not understand all the words, but they love singing it!) For example, change "lords leaping" to "computers beeping."

■ Make a gift for the birds, using a feeder made of a milk carton and hung from a tree that can be easily observed from inside. Cheerios, strung on a string and hung from an outside tree attract winter birds, also.

With all this excitement, it should be easier to see the wonders of December through a child's eyes. You must remember that she has only experienced a few winters and to her all that is old hat to us is still new and fresh and wonderful. Feel the newness and specialness of this holiday, and it will be almost as it was when you were five!

HOLIDAY CRAFTS

SNOW JAR

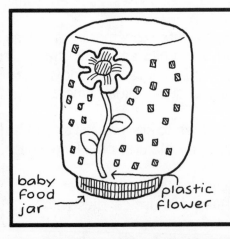

baby food jar → plastic flower

1. Cut a 2" x 2" piece of aluminum foil into tiny squares.
2. Place flower into jar upside down.
3. Place foil squares into jar and fill jar to overflowing with water.
4. Close tightly and shake.

SPONGE PRINTS

1. Place a paper cut-out on a piece of paper.
2. Sponge tempera paint all over.
3. Let dry. Remove cut-outs for a silhouette look.

CUT-OUTS

PAPER STOCKING

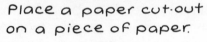

1. Cut 2 large stocking shapes from paper. Punch holes through both parts all around.
2. Wrap 1 end of a piece of yarn with tape and use yarn to lace up sides.
3. Fill with hand drawn toys

34

GIFTS OF FOOD

YUMMY TABLE TOP TREE

1. Use a cone-shaped ice cream cone turned upside down.

2. Combine 1/4 cup margarine, 2 tsp. milk, 2 cups confectionary sugar and green food coloring.

3. Frost cone and trim with raisins, nuts, and mini-marshmallows.

GRAHAM CRACKER HOUSE

1. Make a ROYAL FROSTING by beating 3 egg whites to a frothy foam and add 1 lb. confectionary sugar and a few drops of lemon juice.

2. Attach graham crackers to empty milk cartons with frosting.

3. Frost crackers and trim with nuts, candy, raisins, and chocolate chips.

PEANUT BUTTER SNOWBALLS

1. Combine 1 cup peanut butter with 1/2 cup dry milk powder, and a few Tblsp. honey to moisten.

2. Chill mixture 1/2 - 1 hour.

3. Roll into balls and roll balls in shredded coconut.

ORNAMENTS

GLITTER ORNAMENTS

1. Glue glitter onto pinecones, cardboard shapes, and styrofoam balls.

2. HINT: Put glue in a styrofoam meat tray. Put glitter into another. Roll object in glue and then in glitter.

3. Add ribbon or yarn to hang ornaments.

BREAD DOUGH ORNAMENTS

1. Mix together: 4 cups flour, 1 cup salt, 1½ cups warm water.

2. Knead 10 minutes. Keep covered in plastic wrap.

3. Form shapes using water to join pieces of dough.

4. Place on cookie sheets. Bake at 300°F for 1-1½ hours.

5. Paint on features with acrylic paint. Coat with polyurethane or spray acrylic.

TIN ORNAMENTS

1. Draw designs on aluminum pie plates, roasting pans or t.v. dinner trays.

2. Using scissors, cut out designs

3. Hammer nail holes all around design.

4. Put a string through 1 hole to hang the ornament.

TAKE A HOLIDAY FIELD TRIP

KATHLEEN ALLEN MEYER

Children love parties, and so do lonely oldsters. Try putting the two together at a holiday party in a nursing home. It can turn out to be one of the most successful field trips of the year. It is also one that requires several weeks of advance planning. I know, since we organized a party at my school.

First, we called for permission to visit the nursing home and also to ask about the number of men and women patients. Each patient was to receive a large pine cone Christmas tree for his or her meal tray. To make this, the children coated the cones with Elmer's Glue using small brushes, and added beads and glitter.

Once these were finished, the children made old-fashioned paper chains and cardboard and styrofoam ornaments for our "Giving Tree," a small living pine tree, placed on a low table. This was to be taken to the nursing home the day of our field trip. Each child hung her ornament and placed her gift underneath the tree.

When we first decided to take this field trip, we talked about the people we would see, that most of them were as old or older than the children's grandparents and not well enough to go to the store to buy things for themselves. We talked of how nice it would be if each child did little jobs around the house—taking out the garbage or setting the table—and earned change to buy a small present, like pretty soap or a pen, for a special friend in the nursing home. A patient's name was given to each child.

Parents already had been informed about the trip in our newsletter. They helped the children earn money for the project and choose a gift. Almost every child brought in a wrapped gift for the "Giving Tree." The few that did not were given a package to put under it, too.

For two weeks before the trip, our weekly cooking lessons were given over to baking sessions. Children love to cut out and decorate cookies. These were frozen until the day of the visit.

Also, the children had been practicing songs to sing at the party. They practiced on their rhythm instruments, too.

The big day finally arrived. Parents had volunteered to drive and to help, if needed. But, the children were the stars! They sang and they played. Many gnarled fingers tapped along to the tune of "Jingle Bells." And then, each child found her special friend to whom she gave the pine cone tree and present. Many eyes were misty as the new friends talked with each other. Last of all, each child passed a small tray of cookies.

As we left the room for school, the children sang "We Wish You a Merry Christmas." Some of the patients joined in. It had not only been a fun time for everyone, but it taught the children that happiness comes from giving and sharing with others.

HOLIDAYS + FAMILIES = A PARTY

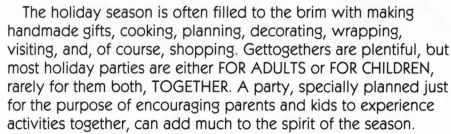

SHERRY BURRELL

The holiday season is often filled to the brim with making handmade gifts, cooking, planning, decorating, wrapping, visiting, and, of course, shopping. Gettogethers are plentiful, but most holiday parties are either FOR ADULTS or FOR CHILDREN, rarely for them both, TOGETHER. A party, specially planned just for the purpose of encouraging parents and kids to experience activities together, can add much to the spirit of the season.

A Parent-Child party puts the focus on families, cooperation, togetherness, giving of oneself, forgiveness, sharing joys, love, peace, and happiness. Here are some thoughts on organization and preparation.

■ Begin by talking to the children about what kinds of things they would enjoy doing with their parents. Help them plan how to invite their parents, and involve them in making signs, invitations, notices, or "tickets" to the event.

■ Be sure that all preliminary notices inform parents that this will be a party at which they will be expected to do activities and play together with the children.

■ Consider arranging for a short magic show or puppet show for parents and their children to enjoy together.

■ Provide a handout to give parents as they arrive at the party. Present a time schedule; state expectations clearly; and appeal to their memories of childhood to get them into the spirit of "play."

■ Set up activity areas around the room with signs, stating the number of parent-child teams that may be there at any one time. Make it clear how many activities may reasonably be attempted in the allotted time period, so that the teams may plan what they want to do together.

■ Plan some craft activities, such as making puppets, ornaments, cards, wreaths, wall hangings, looped potholders, cookie tins, pencil holders, centerpieces, or placemats. Be sure to provide ALL needed materials, as well as clear instructions on what can be done with them.

■ Set up an activity center, focused on encouraging teams to work together to plan holiday gifts and surprises for others.

For example, they might make "gift certificates" to be given together to loved ones, good for "one free back rub," "two free chores," "three big hugs"...Or, teams might write special little poems or make short books of illustrated messages to give as gifts.

■ Consider introducing the fun of playing "Secret Santa." Encourage the teams to think up little gifts or notes to leave as surprises for someone they know. These can be made right at the party. Be sure to tell them that the point of the game is that no one else ever knows who the "Secret Santa" was! Through this secret excitement, parents and children experience the joy of giving, without expecting anything in return.

■ Another idea is to have one staff person stationed with an instant developing camera, ready to take pictures of the teams. It is especially fun when the teams "dress up" in dramatic play outfits to have their pictures taken together. Teams then can take the pictures and make popsicle frames to put them in (or laminate them, or make cardboard frames).

■ If the children have a favorite holiday story they enjoy, consider adapting it into a play, in which the teams become one character together. Each team has one or two short lines to say to make the play come to life. In this type of "play," there is no audience, rather everyone joins in the act!

These are a few ideas for parent-child holiday parties. There is no limit to the ideas your class can come up with.

CREATIVE CRAFTS: DEC.26-JAN.1

KATHY FAGGELLA

We have suggested here various activities for children to create from items probably found around the home during the holiday season. You may wish to send these ideas home to parents.

Holiday Collage

You'll Need:
• piece of wrapping paper
• pieces of ribbon
• tinsel
• glitter
• cutouts from Christmas cards
• glue

What to Do:
1. Let each child glue on bits of this and that to the wrapping paper.
2. Date and have child sign collage to keep for years to come.

Sewing Cards

You'll Need:
• holiday greeting cards
• yarn
• tape
• hole puncher

What to Do:
1. Cut off the cover on a card.
2. Punch holes around design in a simple way.
3. Cut an 18" long piece of yarn and wrap one end in tape. Make a knot at opposite end.
4. Let child "sew" by going up and down through holes.

Popcorn Pictures

You'll Need:
• popped popcorn
• white glue
• heavy paper

What to Do:
1. Have child glue popcorn down onto paper to form a design, figure, or winter scene.
2. Use crayons or markers to add details, if desired. (Optional: you can color popped popcorn by dipping pieces into a cup with diluted food colors, then drying with towels.)

Wishbone Book Mark

You'll Need:
• one turkey, chicken, or cornish hen wishbone, scrubbed clean
• acrylic paint (we like gold)
• 18'' of ½'' wide grosgrain ribbon
What to Do:
1. Brush acrylic paint onto wishbone. Let dry.
2. Tie one end of ribbon in a small bow.
3. Tie other end to wishbone.

Empty Box Sculpture

You'll Need:
• all sizes of gift boxes
• white, tacky glue
• paint (optional)
What to Do:
1. Let children build their own sculptures by gluing gift boxes together.
2. Encourage them to decorate the sculptures with painted-on designs.

Winter Wonderland Pictures

You'll Need:
• dark green or blue construction paper
• white poster paint
• old toothbrush
• small evergreen branch
• glitter
• white glue (Elmer's)
What to Do:
1. Place evergreen branch on paper.
2. Dip toothbrush in paint. Hold brush in one hand and draw thumb across it with the other hand. It will splatter paint on paper. Continue until you see the outline of the branch against a white background.
3. Let paint dry. Then, dab white glue onto white paint and sprinkle glitter on it.

-WISHBONE BOOKMARK -

HAPPY NEW YEAR! ◆ KATHY FAGGELLA

Plan a small New Year's celebration to share with your children. Young children really enjoy being included in such a grown-up holiday.

Make the favors on the next page ahead of time, serve something "bubbly" to drink and Three Kings' Cake, play games, and have everyone contribute to a "Year's Past" mural. Just enough to make it memorable, but not too much for little merrymakers!

Year's Past Mural

Spread out a large piece of paper and have everyone draw something they remember from the past year—the trip to the zoo, a puppet show, making applesauce. It will be fun remembering together!

Balloon Games

■ Kick a balloon to the finish line.
■ Hop with a balloon between your knees to the finish line.
■ Blow a balloon to the finish line or roll it with your nose.
■ Stomp and pop all the balloons with a timer set at two minutes.

Three Kings' Cake

Children can help bake this special cake to enjoy at your celebration. Use your favorite cake recipe or mix and stir three whole almonds into the batter. Bake as usual. Frost the cake and decorate with wedges of green and red apples around the edges to resemble a crown. Use candies or lemon rind for additional decoration.

As you eat the cake, the three people who find the almonds in their pieces are the three kings (or queens). They get to wear foil crowns for the rest of the party.

3 KINGS CAKE
(3 ALMONDS HIDDEN IN BATTER)

NEW YEAR'S FAVORS

TIN PLATE RATTLERS

YOU'LL NEED:

 tape

 handful of dried beans

 stapler

 paper streamers

 2 aluminum foil pie plates

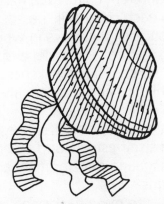

WHAT TO DO:

1. Place dried beans in 1 plate.

2. Invert second plate over first and staple around.

3. Tape paper streamers to center of 1 plate.

NOISEMAKER CRACKERS

YOU'LL NEED:

 1 frozen orange juice can

 tissue paper

 curly ribbon

 wrapped candy or trinkets

 glue

 scissors

WHAT TO DO:

1. Remove both ends of orange juice can.

2. Measure tissue paper so it extends 3" beyond the 2 ends of the can and completely wraps around.

3. Glue tissue paper around can and tie 1 end with ribbon. Fringe with scissors.

4. Fill can with candy and close the open end with ribbon. Fringe that end.

MARTIN LUTHER KING'S BIRTHDAY

SYLVIA MALM

This is a good time to help your children understand, accept, and appreciate the differences among people. This seems to be the spirit of Dr. King's philosophy and of this holiday. Because of satellites, computers, and television, children today are aware of the whole world. However, appreciating different languages, customs, and ideas does not come easily. We, as teachers, can help young children develop an understanding of different races and cultures. This understanding will help them deal with the different kinds of people they will meet.

How does a teacher introduce different cultures to her class? Children often make comments on each other's likenesses and differences. Encourage them to notice all the ways in which they are alike and different—hair color, texture, and style; eye color and shape; skin color; height; and so on. Physical likenesses and differences are most obvious to children and they are always interested in themselves and each other at this age.

Classroom activities can be built around this self-interest. The main idea is to increase each child's self-esteem and awareness of others, but other benefits are language development and a growing ability to make comparisons.

One of the first activities we do is to make handprints and footprints. You'll need two colors of tempera paint and one adult to cover the child's hand or foot using a brush. Make two sets of prints—one for home and the other to put on the wall at school. Some children will be reluctant to get dirty. Show them how easily the paint washes off, but don't force them to join in. They will learn by watching, too.

A photograph of each child on the wall makes that person feel special. Photographs of children and families from other cultures help children become aware of and more comfortable with differences.

We also discuss languages. When a child is using Vietnamese or Spanish in my school, I identify the language being spoken. The children become aware of other languages and sometimes learn a few words in the new language. They accept and appreciate each other's ability in another language. We also sing songs in English, Spanish, and Vietnamese so that all children in the class will have a chance to sing in their own language. The children's parents are a great resource for simple children's songs and have been willing to teach them to us.

Sometimes children let you know that they are aware of cultural and racial differences—and that they are uncomfortable with them. This is probably one of the most difficult times for a teacher. Use children's comments as a stepping stone to discussions. Be honest and offer simple information.

CELEBRATE PURIM

RUTH A. MUSKINOW

Costume Patterns

GOWN- CUT 2 PIECES AND SEW

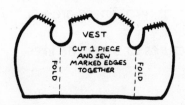

VEST
CUT 1 PIECE AND SEW MARKED EDGES TOGETHER
FOLD   FOLD

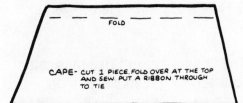

FOLD

CAPE- CUT 1 PIECE. FOLD OVER AT THE TOP AND SEW. PUT A RIBBON THROUGH TO TIE

The holiday of Purim celebrates the heroic rescue of the Jewish community from the wicked plot of Haman, a minister in ancient Persia. A story scroll tells the tale of the evil Haman, heroic Mordecai, beautiful Esther, and the weak King Achashverosh. It is traditionally read to the accompaniment of noisemakers shaken by children and adults in colorful costumes. This celebration is a marvelous experience in the Early Childhood classroom. It can be found in the Book of Esther in the Bible and in *Jewish Days and Holidays* by Greer Fay Cashman.

You can transform your dramatic play area by painting a large packing case with bright colors and adding towers to make it seem more like a Persian palace. Provide a throne and props.

The custom of making loud noises to drown out the name of evil Haman during the reading of the Purim story requires rattles of different kinds. Explore percussive sound in the classroom. Gather many containers of different shapes and prepare sand, pebbles, beans, rice, and buttons to fill your Purim noisemakers. Let children listen to the different sounds. Seal some of the containers and have children try to match the sounds. Encourage them to paint or decorate the noisemakers with cloth and paper.

Traditional costumes for the story characters can be made in school if you provide bright fabrics and trimmings and simple brown paper patterns.

Broom handles can be equipped with horse heads cut from brown paper, stapled and stuffed with torn newspaper, with tails of yarn or cloth strips. A simple tri-cornered paper hat will identify Haman and his wicked friends and pipe cleaners attached to yarn beards will hook behind the ears of each little Mordecai.

Many different kinds of puppets help extend the fun of the Purim story. Stuffed socks with button eyes and noses; nylon hose, stretched over a wire hanger frame, with a painted face; a potato face with a hole dug out for the finger that moves the head; all become puppets that tell funny or silly stories.

Traditionally, families exchange delicious treats in decorated baskets. These include three-cornered Haman cakes filled with poppy seeds or fruit preserves. These goodies must be shared and should include giving of one's self by reaching out to others in school and perhaps to older people living in the community. Costumed children singing holiday songs and carrying the treats they have prepared in a visit to a local residence for senior citizens generates a mutually satisfactory experience when carefully planned by a teacher alert to the needs of both groups.

VALENTINE'S DAY PARTY

KATHY FAGGELLA

A Valentine's Day party can be a lot of fun and generate so much love in the process! The following are some fun-loving heart projects to make your Valentine's Day party a huge success.

Making Hearts

This is a simple way for a young child to make his own Valentine's Day heart for someone special. First, help the child fold a piece of paper in half. Show him how to hold folded paper in one hand with thumb over fold, slanting upward. Then, have him—or you—trace around the thumb with a pencil. Have the child remove his thumb and cut on traced line. Let him decorate with sparkles, lace, ribbons, and so on.

"I Love" Book

Have each child put together a special "I Love" Book filled with pictures of the things he likes best.
You'll Need:
• four sheets of red, white, and pink 8½" x 11" construction paper
• white yarn
What to Do:

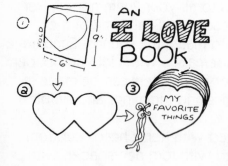

1. With children, fold each piece of paper in half and trace a large heart onto it—making sure the left side of the heart overlaps the fold slightly. Cut out. Repeat with all four sheets of paper.
2. You will have eight hearts in pairs of two. These are your pages. Fold together and tie with yarn.
3. Let each child draw or cut out pictures of things he likes. Include photos, if possible.

GAMES

What's a party without games? Here are some "Heart" games to play at the party.

Musical Hearts

This game should really be called "hug-a-heart!" Like Musical Chairs, children dance around and listen for the music to stop. Yet, here's the difference—when the music stops, children must stand on a large heart-shaped piece of newspaper on the floor. Start with as many hearts as there are children. The fun begins as one heart shape is removed each time the music starts again. Now, children must share heart shapes when the music stops. Of course, the best part comes at the end when all the children are hugging each other in order to stay on the one last heart shape! NO ONE SHOULD BE ELIMINATED FROM THIS GAME!

Tiddly Wink Hearts

This game encourages small motor coordination. It also may be used for scoring points and counting.

You'll Need:
- card stock, oaktag, or posterboard (large sheet)
- tacky glue
- tape
- scissors
- marker
- poker chips or large flat buttons
- optional: beans as counters

What to Do:

1. Cut two strips of posterboard to 1½" x 20". Place one strip on top of other.

2. Tape securely together on one end of both strips.

3. Separate strips and bend taped ends to form top of heart.

4. Draw open ends together and tape to form bottom of heart.

5. Use tacky glue to glue this large heart in place on a larger sheet of posterboard.

6. Make two more hearts—one heart, using two 1½" x 15" strips, and another, a small one, using two 1½" x 10" strips. Glue medium and small hearts inside large heart so that bottom points meet.

7. Trim background posterboard to heart shape. Use a marker to write the number "1" inside the large heart, "2" inside the medium heart, and "3" inside the small heart.

8. Use poker chips or buttons to flip into heart shapes. Use beans to keep score: one bean for each point scored.

A party is not complete unless there are some type of refreshments served. Why not serve Peanut Butter and Jelly Heart Cookies? The recipe is on page 48.

HEART COOKIES

YOU'LL NEED:

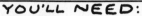 heart-shaped cookie cutters ½ cup margarine ¼ cup shortening ¾ cup peanut butter  1 cup sugar 1 egg   1 small jar—raspberry jam

 1 tsp. vanilla  2 Tblsp. milk 3 cups flour   rolling pin cookie sheet mixer cooling rack plastic knife

WHAT TO DO:

 1. Beat margarine, shortening, and peanut butter well. Add egg and beat well.

 2. Add sugar, vanilla, and flour with milk.

3. Chill 2 hours or more.

 4. Roll dough on lightly floured board to ¼" thick.

 5. Cut out heart shapes with cookie cutters.

 6. Place on a lightly greased cookie sheet. Bake at 350°F for 8-10 minutes (until slightly browned).

 7. Remove to cooling rack.

 8. Spread 1 tsp. jam on a cookie and cover with another for the peanut butter and jelly sandwich effect.

HAVE A LITTLE ♡ VE BOX

SPECIAL CARRY BOX

YOU'LL NEED:
- felt tip markers or crayons
- a deep cardboard carton
- glue
- scissors
- construction paper

WHAT TO DO:

1. Cut out carton as shown and then cover with construction paper.

2. Decorate with markers or crayons.

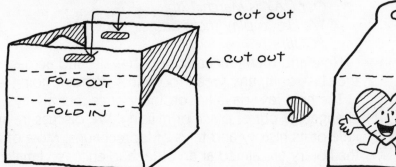 

cut out

← cut out

FOLD OUT

FOLD IN

 ITEMS TO INCLUDE IN THE BOX:

1.  A tiny package of 4 or 5 SUNFLOWER SEEDS for somebody to plant and feel good about as they watch them grow.

2. A BALLOON which has been blown-up and has had "I LOVE YOU" written on it with a ball point pen and then has been deflated.

3.  A tracing of the CHILD'S HAND with a heart shape cut out of the center.

4.  A COUPON for 1 hug, 1 kiss, etc. can be added to the box. children can give the coupons to family members who, in turn, cash them in.

—ONE COUPON—
FOR: ♡ FROM:
GOOD FOR 1 HUG, 1 KISS, ETC.

ST PATRICK'S DAY

JEANNINE PEREZ

We begin St. Patrick's Day well in advance in my classroom. I usually have a unit on fairy and folk tales after the February holidays and we talk about "once about a time...s" introducing the concept of make-believe.

About a week before the big day, the children come to the class and on the outside of the door, they find a big poster in different shades of green. Little green faces peek over mushroom houses and there is spidery lettering with this message:

GUESS WHO WAS HERE
We live in mushrooms.
Our beds are made of grass.
We eat berries and drink morning dew.
Our DAY is March 17th.
We like to play tricks on...
YOU!!!

Here and there, meandering up walls and across windows in the classroom, tiny green footprints wander, going—no place!

The next few days are ordinary ones, but always, something is changed or out of place or missing. We discuss Ireland, tell a little of its history and tales of leprechauns. Most of the books in the library are aimed at an older audience, so I make up my own versions. We paint huge rainbows on the bulletin board and make mushroom houses and tiny leprechauns for the bottom.

Leprechauns can be made many ways. Sometimes, the children merely draw their own versions. Sometimes, we use cups from papier-maché egg cartons—one for the hat, one for the head—spool or box for body, and green yarn for hair. They can be made from lunch bags stuffed with newspapers, secured and turned upside down. Markers, paints, construction paper scraps, and crayons can be used for faces, buttons, belts, and hats.

We also cut shamrocks from thin sponges or old terry toweling—one for each child—moisten it, and plant alfalfa or grass seed on it. I use sample paint chip cards in varying shades of green and we decide which is the darkest, lightest, dullest, and brightest—and which green shade is our personal favorite.

On March 16, the children find another note on the door. Shaped like a giant shamrock, it says:

TOP O' THE MORNING!
We were here again—in the middle of the night.
We cleaned your art center—it was a TERRIBLE sight!
Please leave us some crackers, to eat, on the table.
And we'll visit again, tonight, if we're able!

With good fortune and some reinforcement, this note should be good for some concentrated clean up of the center—and perhaps, a few crackers for tired, hungry teachers!

The next day is the big day and, like all special days, is stimulating enough that cool-down ideas must be incorporated at strategic times. I get Irish records from the library to dance to, and plan for ample physical activities as outlets for the excitement.

When the children come in, they see, first of all, one last green poster covering almost the whole door.

> *It's back to our forest—*
> *Where everything's green.*
> *We hide under leaves—so we are never seen.*
> *We'll come again next year—*
> *If we may.*
> *And, we wish you for now—*
> *HAPPY ST. PAT'S DAY!!!*
> *P.S. Look for our magic dust.*

Inside, lights and windows are covered with green tissue, small green footprints covered with green glitter are everywhere, and a small burlap bag is stapled to the end of the rainbow. (The treasure can be silver candy kisses or gold foil-wrapped packages of raisins.)

Sometime during the day, we have a shamrock hunt (much like an Easter egg hunt). I usually put a number on each shamrock, so the children can decide which shamrock has the largest number and wins. At our center, everyone is a winner and we sit down to Mulligan stew, Irish soda bread (made the day before), green apple juice, and lots of green salad!

EASTER SCIENCE

PATRICK GINNANE

Each spring, Mother Nature brings us bright colors in birds, buds, and blossoms. The pastels of spring help make the world a prettier place.

We join the natural world in celebrating spring. The Easter egg is one traditional symbol of this annual rebirth.

Turning to traditional crafts, you and your children can create natural dyes for your Easter egg decorating. By making their own dyes, children are learning about the additional properties of familiar foods, and one of the processes by which we put some of nature's color into our own lives.

To prepare each dye, *you'll need:*
• salt
• water
• saucepan
• onion skins or saffron (yellow)
• coffee (brown)
• beets (red)
• red cabbage (purple)
• blueberries (blue)

What to Do:
1. Chop or grind the basic ingredient.
2. Add it to a small saucepan of water with a pinch of salt.
3. Bring to a boil.
4. Simmer for 20 minutes. Strain.

Experiment with quantities. You will need a very strong solution to get a deep color.

Try to increase the children's sense of the natural source of the ingredients by using fresh whole ingredients, whenever possible. You can add to the activity with photos of coffee plantation and beets in a garden.

Spring, with the promise of fair weather, nature study, and outdoor experiences of all kinds, once again invites us to make scientific discoveries. A "natural" part of this exploration of nature is, of course, the spring flower and vegetable garden. Sprouting the seeds indoors first not only provides for an earlier start, but also allows children to observe more closely the daily progress of their plantings.

A less traditional, but equally colorful, garden is the "Crystal Garden." To grow your own, prepare a solution of ½ cup salt, ½ cup water, ½ cup laundry blueing, and 1 tablespoon of ammonia. Place some crumpled paper towels in the bottom of a goldfish bowl or other large, clear glass container. Pour the solution into the bowl and add several drops of food coloring. In a few days, your beautiful crystal flowers will bloom in the pretty pastel shades of spring.

52

CAKE IN A BASKET

YOU'LL NEED:

 1 shallow 8" OR 9" round basket with handle

 ·OR· 13"x9" oblong basket

jelly beans

 1 carrot or spice cake mix empty jar   green food coloring

1 yd. ribbon cooling rack 1 cup shredded coconut

 baking pan- similar in size and shape to basket

 white frosting- of your choice

OR MAKE YOUR OWN
1. mix 6 oz. cream cheese
   3 cups confectionary sugar
   2 tsp. vanilla
2. Beat well.

WHAT TO DO:

1.
Bake the cake according to package directions. Make sure you bake it in a pan that will later enable it to fit into a basket.

2.
Remove cake from pan(s). Set on rack and put into freezer for 1-2 hours.

3.
Meanwhile, line basket with aluminum foil.

4.
Place frozen cake into foil-lined basket. You may have to cut 13"x9" cake in half for it to fit into basket easier.

5.
Frost cake. Shake coconut with a few drops of green food coloring in a jar. Place this "grass" on top of frosting.

6.
Hide the jelly bean "eggs" in the "grass." Tie a ribbon on the handle.

53

MOTHER'S DAY LUNCH

SARA A. SALANCY

The week before Mother's Day actually occurs, Christ and Holy Trinity Preschool in Westport, CT., has a special luncheon and each child in the four-year-old class gets to celebrate his special relationship with his parent.

This event is planned for and eagerly awaited weeks in advance. In fact, the parents always seem as excited as the children! What busy parent would not like to sit down beside her child at a beautiful table to eat a meal her child has made and eagerly serves and shares? And, all this in a pleasant setting of other parents enjoying a special part of parenting!

While we do set aside a Saturday morning for "Dad's Day," it seems especially appropriate to "turn tables on" those largely responsible for meal preparation at home. And, we have found that even the most hard-pressed mothers can get extra time for the Mother's Day Lunch.

For the children, our celebration means lots of work, fun, learning, and a great feeling of accomplishment. At the same time, the children have the joy of making a surprise—much easier to manage in the school setting than at home. Finally, this is a special meal for this one child and his mother (and others similarly bonded); siblings, fathers, and friends are not invited, though an exception can be made for a visiting grandmother.

For the teacher, the planning must be done well in advance. Is the classroom big enough? Do tables and chairs need to be borrowed from friends and family? Which day is most convenient in terms of the children's schedules and the needs of the rest of the school? What kinds of food can the children prepare themselves safely, inexpensively, and in advance? Are certain dishes inappropriate, considering the children's cultural backgrounds?

Trying not to give the children too much lead time, we begin by making invitations whiich are hard to lose or overlook. The children make a "flower" with the announcement taped firmly around the bottom of the "pot"—we use a styrofoam egg cup flower, a pipe cleaner stem, and some clay to anchor it inside a sturdy plastic cup.

Next, we discuss the menu. Making tossed salad means getting to tear up lettuce, chop—with a plastic knife—celery, green pepper, tomatoes, carrots, and cucumber, and decorate it all with bean sprouts. Making Jello fruit salad means not only the fun of making Jello, but of giving Mom the fruits the child does not really want in his Jello. The children mix up the wholesome ingredients for the miniature muffins and admit that Mom likes things that are not too sweet—the children always like the muffins, too, somehow. Our main course is usually a

tuna—macaroni salad, mixed in a huge bowl by the children.

As none of the food can be prepared too far in advance, the children make placemats and placecards and assemble place settings while waiting for "cooking" days. Using special fabric crayons, they make pictures on paper which we iron onto rectangles of pink sheeting fabric. The paper picture serves as the child's placemat, while the fabric one is for Mom. Another day, each child wraps a plastic knife, fork, and spoon into a big paper napkin and, with little help from a teacher, ties it up in yarn.

On the morning of our Mother's Day Lunch, each child sets a place for himself and Mom complete with placecards. Then, with the classroom filled with tables and chairs for twice our usual number, we go off to sing, to hear stories, or, best of all, play outside.

When the mothers arrive, usually early, we bring them into a spare room and sing some love and friendship songs for them. Once the children have calmed down a bit, they lead the mothers to their places. After we sing the "Johnny Appleseed Grace," the feast begins. Although the food is set out on the tables in big bowls and plates, there is still a chance for the children to help their mothers—our limited space prevents the children from fully waiting on their mothers. When children and mothers finish, they have full tummies and placemats to take home. We, teachers, breathe a sigh of relief, but feel, as we do every year, that it was all worth it.

The next day, we feel more certain of the benefits of "Mother's Day Lunch." The children are still beaming over their part in it and their mothers stop by or leave notes to tell us how much it meant to them. In fact, the feedback is so positive that we must keep reminding everyone that Dad has his "Day" and the real "Mother's Day" is yet to come—on Sunday.

ARBOR DAY

JANET HOROWITZ

There are many reasons why trees are lovely, lovable, and such important symbols—of life, strength, growth, and endurance. Young children can begin to understand these concepts if we help them to experience trees in their daily lives. Arbor Day is the perfect time to begin.

Love and appreciation of trees begin by getting to know them. With people, it feels good to see a familiar face. The same thing can happen with a tree. If you help a child become familiar with one or many trees, she will always feel as if she has a friend. Let each child "adopt" one tree in your play yard, neighborhood park, on the street—or she might even plant her own sapling.

It's not enough to just look at the tree; encourage each child to get close to her tree by:
• Hugging it. How far do her arms reach around it? Measure with a string. Paste the string on paper.
• Kissing it. Smell its bark, leaves, pine cones, flowers, and acorns.
• Exploring it carefully with her eyes. Then, let her use a handlens.
• Exploring it carefully with her hands and feet. Have each child close her eyes and feel the bark, leaves, twigs, and buds.
• Finding out who lives in the tree. Trees give homes to animals. Here's what to look for: nests; wet holes for mosquitos, tree frogs, and polliwogs; and dry holes where you may find owls, woodpeckers, racoons, and beehives.

With each child, find out as much as you can about her tree. Keep the findings in a book—a big class tree book or individual ones. Have each child draw a picture of her tree. Paste a leaf, twig, and seed from the tree on a page. Include the string measurement. Make a bark rubbing by pressing a piece of paper against the bark and rubbing hard on it with a crayon or wax candle. Photograph each child with her tree—if possible over the course of several seasons.

Make sure that the children enjoy their trees. Encourage them to:
• Climb on low branches
• Listen to the wind blowing through the leaves
• Lie on the ground and look up through the leaves

Return to the friendly trees many times throughout the year. Watch them grow and change. It's a wonderful way to celebrate life.

THE FOURTH OF JULY

FRANCINE JARONCYZK

Another Independence Day rolls around and once again you are faced with the unhappy prospect of trying to plan a celebration with your children that does justice to this historical event, engages the children's interest and curiosity, and takes into account the wonderful outdoors of summertime.

Why not plan a birthday party for the U.S.A. that includes a parade and some outdoor summer Olympics?

HAVE A PARADE

Make your own drums, cymbals, and horns with everyday household items. Of course, use any rhythm band instruments available to you to back up your homemade ones. Add to your music one large flag or small ones for everyone.

You'll Need:
- fingerpaint paper
- masking tape
- cardboard tube from wrapping paper roll
- red crepe paper
- glue
- blue fingerpaint

What to Do:

1. First, arrange about four pieces of fingerpaint paper into a rectangle with the longest side being as long as the carboard tube. Tape the pieces together, using masking tape only on one side.

2. Cut 13 pieces of red crepe paper streamers the length of the longest side of your rectangle. Glue them horizontally to the paper to make the stripes of the flag.

3. Fingerpaint one piece of paper blue and cut it into a perfect square. This will become the blue field of your flag. Glue the square to the upper lefthand corner of your rectangle.

4. Trace or draw stars on white paper and help your children to cut these out and glue them to the blue field.

5. Roll the top of the flag around the wrapping paper tube and tape securely with masking tape. Two children can carry this flag in your parade.

Make batons for twirling with cardboard paper towel tubes. Decorate each tube by painting it and gluing on glitter or sequins. If you are using glitter, cover the tube with clear contact paper to protect the children's eyes from loose, flying glitter. Stuff colored tissue paper into both ends of the tube.

Large American Flag

Batons

SOME BALLOON GAMES—

KICK IT

HOP WITH IT

BLOW IT

FINISH LINE

OUTDOOR SUMMER OLYMPICS

Some popular games to arrange are the following: three-legged races, wheelbarrow races, an obstacle course race, pass-the-raw-egg race, and pop-the-balloon race.

Also, you can have a Shoe Hunt Race. Have everyone take off their shoes and place them into a pile. Blow a whistle to signal the beginning of the hunt, and have children race to the pile, find their shoes, put them on, tie them, and race back. You may wish to have tie-on, velcro, and slip-on shoe races separately. Group children together with similar abilities, so no one feels like a loser.

Play Pitch the Ball into the Shape. Cut shapes into the bottom of a large box. Standing at a given distance from the box, children can take turns pitching a soft ball or bean bag into specific shapes.

Make up ribbon and safety pin awards for everyone who participated in the Olympics.

YOU'RE TERRIFIC!

ONE WONDERFUL KID

WOW YOU DID IT!

SEASONAL CELEBRATIONS

A TREE FOR ALL MONTHS

 SEPTEMBER has the tree covered with multi-colored leaves, numbered 1-30. Each day we take off a leaf (taking turns sending them home with the children). We talk about September, what we can expect to see, hear, and feel in this month.

 OCTOBER finds a few owls and cats in the almost bare tree, a big harvest moon in 1 corner, and numbered Jack O'Lanterns. The children enjoy decorating for Halloween and it is just as much fun to see it gradually disassembled.

 **NOVEMBER** has fat turkeys numbered for the days of the month all hiding in the branches of the tree from the cook below. The tree has only a few brown leaves, still hanging on and we compare it with the trees outside that are equally bare.

 DECEMBER brings with it reindeer and Santa's sleigh under the tree. By this time, our tree has a sprinkling of snowflakes caught in its branches and the ground under the tree also is white.

 JANUARY snowmen stand on the hills behind our tree and some hide behind it. Each has a different color scarf. (we talk about colors.) We also talk about what animals do in the winter and a cave can be seen in the background. Each snowman is numbered for the days of the month, ready for the children to take home.

 FEBRUARY has a Valentine Tree with the branches covered with metallic hearts. It is so gaudy and sparkly that we are glad February is a short month and we can plan March's theme.

 MARCH has lambs and lions frisking around our tree, some fluffy clouds in the sky, and a few leaf buds showing on the tree with leprechauns hiding here and there.

 APRIL has added many new and green leaves added, a few raindrops, and a rainbow in the sky. Numbered umbrellas are placed under the tree.

 MAY has our tree covered with pink tissue blossoms and birds.

 JUNE finds our garden of flowers blooming under the tree. Each flower is numbered with the days of June and is ready for picking.

 JULY has flags under the tree and fireworks above it. By this time, the children are making their own suggestions for monthly themes and we incorporate them into the picture.

 **AUGUST** finds the tree covered with apples, ready for picking rosy, and numbered. It is a natural time for including lots of apple activities, cooking with apples, and even apple-head dolls. Our tree has watched us grow for a year and we have enjoyed and appreciated the changes the seasons made in its life.

CELEBRATE AUTUMN

KATHY FAGGELLA

A "Countdown to Fall" chain can be made, from paper strips—a chain link for each day until the first day of fall. On each link, suggest one activity to do to prepare for the changing of summer to fall. Make it simple. Here are some suggestions.

• Collect a flower and put it into a flower press.
• Set out a bunch of washed green grapes in a warm, dry place. In a couple of weeks, they will be raisins.
• See if you can find a squirrel collecting nuts.

When the first day of fall finally arrives, celebrate with a Fall Day Party.

■ Make invitations by gluing pressed flowers and leaves to folded paper.
■ Make decorations from your dried weeds and acorns and clothespin dolls.
■ Serve special snacks like homemade raisins, dried apple rings, popcorn, roasted pumpkin seeds, and cider.
■ Play games:
• **Shadow Tag** Run around outside in the sun. The person who is "it" must step on your shadow!
• **Scavenger Hunt Bingo** Make two or three chart-sized bingo cards. You can use pictures only or add labels. Cover with contact paper. Divide children into teams. They must go out and find items on the bingo card. Then, they bring them back and place items directly on the chart. When the chart is completely covered, the team yells "Bingo."
· Make music. Sing "fall" songs. Make up new words to familiar songs using fall words. ("Old MacDonald Had Orange Leaves.")
· Make a party favor with a few dried apple rings and a stick. The old Native American game of ring and pin is fun and challenging to try. Tie a string to one apple ring and thread on two or three others. Now, tie the other end of the string to the bottom of an eight inch stick. Flip the rings onto the pin.

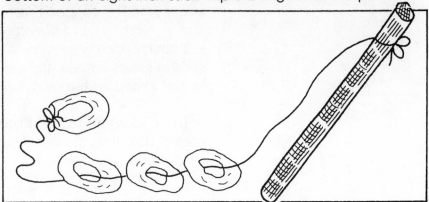

FALL LEARNING FUN

KATHY FAGGELLA

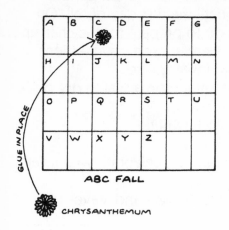

ABC FALL

GLUE IN PLACE

CHRYSANTHEMUM

Celebrate fall with learning activities, which help children discover the joys of the season.

■ Make booklets in "fall" shapes—leaves, Indian corn, pumpkins, apples, the moon. Staple sheets of paper together. Have each child draw pictures and dictate stories for them.

■ Into a large cardboard carton, put a tape recorder—easy enough for children to operate—and five "fall" objects. They could be a sweater, an apple, a cornstalk, a chestnut, and a picture of a butterfly. Have children use these objects to make up a story and dictate it into the tape recorder.

■ Make a large alphabet chart. Have children add a fall item that begins with that letter to each section. For example, M—milkweed pod; C—chrysanthemum.

■ Read many storybooks that show how people and animals deal with the changing seasons.

■ Have "fall" items on your science table. Include a magnifying glass and/or a water microscope.

■ Keep a box with "wind testers" in it—feathers, crepe paper streamers, yarn, schoolmade capes for children to wear outside on a windy day.

■ Have a good quantity of acorns, horse chestnuts, Indian corn, gourds, seed pods, and sunflower seeds available for **math experiences**.

SAMPLES

• Provide a balance scale for children to compare the various weights of the objects.

• Provide egg cartons for children to sort the objects.

• Have children use groups of the same type of object to practice counting.

• Have children put three or four objects of the same type—leaves, pods, gourds—in order of size.

• Add twigs, acorns, small logs to sand play. Add a container—foil-lined box—of clean soil, also.

• Print with leaves, pods, harvest fruits and vegetable sections. Use watercolors and brayers.

• Older children will enjoy making seed jewelry. Soak pumpkin or squash seeds for half an hour and let children string them on heavy thread with a blunt needle.

These ideas for learning projects and experiences all have a fall theme. Use them throughout the year, changing the theme as the season changes.

POT POURRI

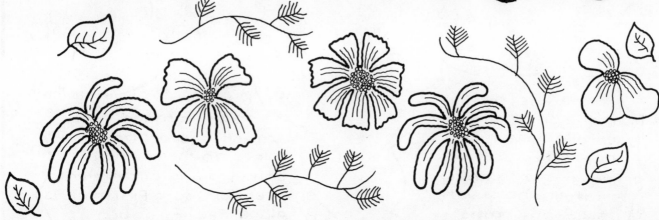

YOU'LL NEED

jar with lid

bowl

teaspoon

orrisroot (available in drug stores and health food stores)

measuring cup

Flower petals and leaves- roses, violets, jasmine, narcissus

herbs- basil leaves, sage, thyme, lavender, lemon verbena

OPTIONAL: spices, cloves, allspice, or cinnamon

WHAT TO DO:

1. Collect flower petals and leaves- roses, violets, jasmine, narcissus.

2. Pick herbs- sage, basil leaves, thyme, lavendar, lemon verbena.

3. Dry petals and herbs on paper in an airy, dry place-out of the sunlight.

4. When dry, mix in a bowl with 1 tsp. of orrisroot to each pint of petals.

5. Add spices, if you wish- cloves, cinnamon, or allspice.

6. Put mixture in a tightly covered jar for 6 weeks. Then, open and make into little pillows or keep in baskets.

63

FUN IN THE SNOW

Have knee races in the snow. When children have their snowsuits on, see who goes faster "running" on their knees. Note the funny paths they make.

Make a maze—mark a starting place. Then, let the child walk in all different directions to a finish place. See if you or another child can get through the maze.

Make 3 snowballs. Let child see you hide a treat like a jellybean in 1 snowball. While he is watching, move the snowballs around. Let child guess which snowball has the treat. Then, let child hide the treat and do the switching around.

Help child build a snowman just his size. Then, let him dress the snowman in his own hat, sweater, and scarf.

FUN OUT OF THE SNOW

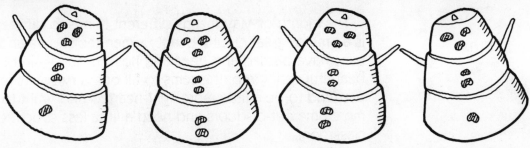

SNOWY DAY PICTURES

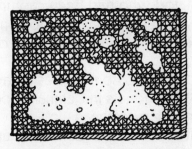

1. Have children mix Ivory Snow Flakes and water with handbeaters until thick and foamy.

2. Then, let them paint with this mixture on blue paper to create a snowy scene.

SNOWMAN SNACKS

1. Provide each child with 3 marshmallows and a toothpick.

2. Let them build model snowmen and add raisins for facial features and buttons.

3. Extra toothpicks can be used for arms.

ICE CRYSTAL PICTURES

1. Have children draw a picture with crayons on a darkish piece of construction paper.

2. Prepare a mixture of equal parts of epsom salts and water.

3. Have children paint the solution over their crayon picture. When paper dries, "ice crystals" will appear.

CELEBRATE SPRING

KATHY FAGGELLA

The month of May means different things to different people. It is a time of great natural beauty when the snows and heavy rains have passed and trees and flowers are again blooming. This beautiful spring rebirth seems to fill our very spirits and outlooks. We tend to be a little more light-hearted and want to spend more time out-of-doors and need a little less structure in the classroom.

May is indeed a merry month! Our ancestors felt very much like we do today. They planned elaborate feasts, parades, dances, and events to celebrate this special month. The Romans had a festival to the goddess Floralia. The Celts in Great Britain celebrated the escape of the sun god who had been captured by the evil spirits in the fall. They also used May Day to honor the anniversary of the death of Robin Hood and his beloved outlaws.

Even today, May Day means cherry blossom dances in Japan, the exchanging of lily of the valley bouquets in Denmark, sports contests in Italy, pine tree planting by sweethearts in Switzerland, and a pole dance at the seedtime festival in Burma!

Many colleges have May festivals that still involve song, dance, flowers, and even hoop rolling. Everyone, in some way, seems to be affected by this special month. So why not plan a celebration?

Use the May Day theme and celebrate the culmination of a year well done. There is a special joy in using one theme and developing all the activities around it. Instead of fragmented activities, you have one activity related to another. You can spend a part of each day making the baskets and flowers and learning the dances. Children are learning many skills, the least of which is that many parts make up a whole. The activities include classifying, comparison, motor skills, as well as following directions and developing social skills. The preparations could be used for a party for themselves or others. Children will be entertained as well as entertaining!

MAY FLOWERS

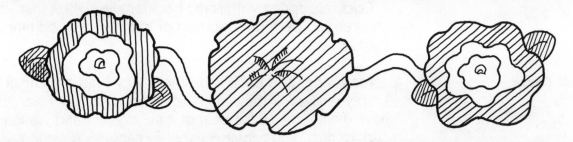

POM-POM FLOWERS

1. Cut several strips of tissue 8"x10" long and 4"-5" wide.

2. With scissors, fringe both long sides.

3. Pulling thumb and forefingers together, bunch up paper from 2 short sides and tape center around pipe cleaner.

FOIL DAISIES

1. Fold a 10"-12" piece of florist foil or aluminum foil in half.

2. Cut scallop edges along side opposite the fold.

3. Gently, bunch up fold and tape around a drinking straw stem.

PIPE CLEANER POSIES

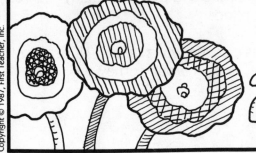

1. Slip circles of colored tissue paper over 1 end of a very fuzzy pipe cleaner. Place many layers of tissue down about ½".

2. Bend pipe cleaners ½" down to hold tissue circles in place and ruffle edges.

SPRING MUSIC AND MOVEMENT

KATHY FAGGELLA

Celebrate spring with some traditional activities that your children can perform for others or just have a good time among themselves.

May Pole Dance

For young children, it is best that they hold a streamer and simply walk or, if they can, skip around the May Pole. You can have them listen to the beat of a tambourine and walk slowly, skip, or hop. You can also signal a change in direction.

Some children can stand in a stationary outside circle, holding streamers, while others move around in a circle inside.

Morris Dance

This old dance was very noisy as dancers clacked wooden boards to help wake up the earth. They leaped high, hoping the crops would grow as tall. They waved handkerchiefs and raised their hands.

Children face a partner and just dance in place, using a jiglike hop. At the same time, they can clack wooden blocks together in time to the music. They wear bells on ankles and wrists as well to increase the noise!

Hoop Rolling

You can use hula hoops, bicycle tires, or green sapling branches, tied in a circle. Children can tie or tape flowers to the INSIDE of the hoop. Hoop rolling is difficult, so do not expect too much. Using a stick to help roll the hoop is NOT recommended because children could fall with it or poke each other.

Waltz of the Flowers

With all the emphasis on flowers in May, children would love to dress up and dance. Create colorful, flower costumes.

You'll Need:
• many scarves or squares of chiffon in varying colors
• ¾'' thick, stretchy waistband elastic
• needle and thread

What to Do:
1. Cut elastic to fit waist, wrists, and as a headband for a child.
2. Sew ends together.
3. Children put on pieces of elastic and tuck in as many scarves as they wish around elastic bands.

They can sway to the music of the waltz in the "Nutcracker Suite," join hands and circle, or spin around. They will look adorable!

MAY BASKETS

PAPER PLATE BASKET

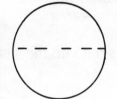

YOU'LL NEED:

- 2 large paper plates
- hole punch
- tape
- pastel yarn pieces
- basket fillers

WHAT TO DO:

1. Cut 1 paper plate in half.

2. Place one half inverted on top of full plate so edges match. Tape together in 2 or 3 places.

3. Use hole punch to make holes around edges of 2 plates. DO NOT make holes along single plate. Punch 2 holes at top for handle.

4. Wind tape around 1 end of a long piece of yarn. Sew through holes to connect plates. Tie off ends.

5. Attach yarn loop as handle. Decorate and fill basket as desired.

PARASOL

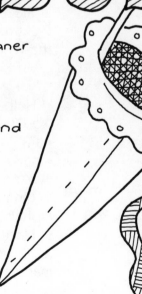

YOU'LL NEED:

- 1 semi-circle of posterboard
- 1 long pipe cleaner
- 1 paper doily
- stapler
- scissors
- collage materials and glue and/or crayons

WHAT TO DO:

1. Cut semi-circle of posterboard and bend to form a cone. Staple along seam.

2. Poke 2 holes near top of cone to insert pipe cleaner as handle.

3. Cut center out of doily and push into cone. Bend edges over cone edges.

4. Color or glue on decorations.

SUMMER PICNIC PARTIES

Picnics, fun, and learning go together. Celebrating summertime often means a brown bag picnic under a tree, on a sandy shore, or along a riverbank. Here are some summertime activities for the "Lunch Bunch." You will find that with some preplanning and preparation, you can turn mealtime into fun and learning.

Nursery Rhyme Prop

Here is a way to bring your favorite rhymes out into the sun.

You'll Need:
• a small card for each child
• markers

What to Do:
1. On each card, draw a "prop" that has to do with a nursery rhyme. Some suggestions are: egg, spider, pumpkin, dish/spoon, pail, dog bone, shoe, ship, star, horn, and so on.
2. Place one in each child's lunch bag.
3. While eating, have children take out their card and guess what nursery rhyme it represents. Ask them to say it. If they have trouble, everyone helps.

Variation: Draw an illustration of a simple nursery rhyme. Have each child look at his own card, then act it out silently, and have others guess the rhyme.

Puzzle Put Together

Did you ever think picnics and puzzles would go together?

You'll Need:
• a cardboard or wooden puzzle or one large picture glued onto heavy cardboard and cut into puzzle shapes

What to Do:
1. Place one puzzle piece into each lunch bag.
2. At mealtime, have children take out their piece and match it to the whole puzzle.

Make-a-Name

Help children learn letters and words in a new way.

You'll Need:
• a 3" by 5" card
• markers

What to Do:
1. On each card, make one letter. Use all the letters of the alphabet.
2. Place one card in each bag.
3. At lunch, have children take out cards and together make as many names as they can.
4. Use one brown bag as a chart to record words with marker.
5. Discuss whose letter is used most. Why?

"Button Rock, Button Rock, Who Has the Button Rock?"

Here is a guessing game that's perfect for a picnic.
You'll Need:
• one small stone
What to Do:
1. Place the small stone into one person's bag.
2. During lunch, tell whoever has the stone to quietly and without letting anyone see it, put it into someone else's bag.
3. When that person finds it, she quietly passes it onto someone else.
4. At the end of lunch, everyone guesses who now has the stone.

Puppets

These creative puppets can be made from the empty lunch bags.
You'll Need:
• markers
• string
• scissors
What to Do:
1. To make a talking puppet, draw a face on the bottom of the bag with markers. A "body" can be drawn with a marker on the rest of the bag. Draw an upper lip on the bottom of the bag and a lower lip on the top side. Work the puppet by placing four fingers in folded bottom and moving them up and down against bag.
2. To make an octopus puppet, tie a string around middle of a bag. With scissors, cut the bottom of the bag into many strips for tentacles. Make a "face" with markers.

Puppet Theater

Cut off ⅓ of bag from opening. Cut a long, narrow rectangle into front side of bag—not seamed side. Use markers to make faces and finger puppets on inside fingertips. Place hand through bag until puppets face out of "stage" window. Make up a play.

Rubbings

Take advantage of your picnic environment for some artwork.
You'll Need:
• one crayon per child
What to Do:
1. Give each child a crayon in their lunch bag.
2. Show children how to tear open bag to make a single, flat sheet.
3. Use brown paper and crayon to make rubbings—bark, cement, monuments, fences.

EASY PICNIC MENUS

 FAVORITE JOBS- CUTTING, SLICING, CHOPPING

 FINGER FOODS

cottage cheese

fresh fruit salad

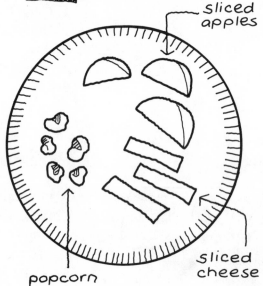

sliced apples

popcorn

sliced cheese

 FUN TO MAKE AND DECORATE

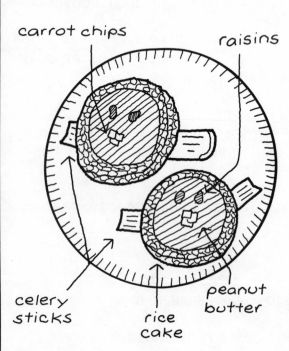

carrot chips

raisins

celery sticks

rice cake

peanut butter

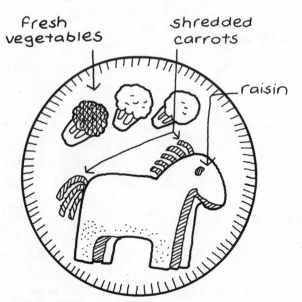

fresh vegetables

shredded carrots

raisin

ANIMAL SANDWICH- make your favorite sandwich filling. Prepare sandwich and use cookie cutters to make shapes.

SPECIAL EVENTS

"CELEBRATE GOOD TIMES..."

KATHY FAGGELLA

Just as the words of the song coax us to "Come and celebrate good times," we'd like to add to that, celebrate any special time. Because that's what celebrations and parties are all about. They are a wonderful break in the regular routine. They give us a chance to recognize someone special or someone's achievements. They give us a chance to work together in a group toward a goal; and even more than all that, celebration times are a good time for learning.

Most children have the opportunity to celebrate their birthday at school. But how about some parties to celebrate other special events in the lives of your children like a new tooth, a new sister or brother, puppies, or achievements like riding a bike or tying shoes? Never pass up a chance to make a child feel important.

Parties may seem like a big deal, but they really aren't that difficult. With a little forethought and preparation, you can assemble a party kit to keep on hand and use for any special occasion.

Everyone in your class should have one celebration party in her honor each year, besides her birthday. Gather together some general party items—a banner, balloons, a celebration cape—and keep them in one place. They should be stored in a closed cabinet or box. Vary the time of the party. Have it at morning or afternoon snack. Vary the style of the party, too. Have an indoor picnic or take a special hike to the park.

Parties can also be used as direct learning situations. What a super opportunity to discuss teeth care and growth when you have a big, one-tooth-missing, grinning face right in front of you! You can use a party to read a book about the many feelings of a new brother or sister. Make a child feel really good and tell about her hints on riding a bike without training wheels. Talk about the care and feeding of a new parakeet. It's guaranteed that this celebration time will sharpen the children's senses and make the learning easy and fun.

And, don't forget little group celebrations—the day you see the first flower of spring, the day you have a work party to straighten up the school, or the day you celebrate all the children with an "I'm Me, I'm Special" party. These are precious, long remembered times. If you doubt that, just remember when...

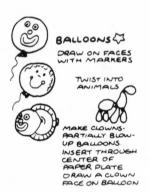

BALLOONS ☆

DRAW ON FACES WITH MARKERS

TWIST INTO ANIMALS

MAKE CLOWNS. PARTIALLY BLOW- UP BALLOONS. INSERT THROUGH CENTER OF PAPER PLATE DRAW A CLOWN FACE ON BALLOON

Happy 5th Birthday, Joshua!

October 1, 1984

"I'M SPECIAL" PARTY

FRANCINE JARONCYZK

Plan a celebration to highlight the uniqueness of each and every child. Help children discover and learn to appreciate the things about themselves that are very special and that make them one of a kind.

HOW TO BEGIN

The day before your celebration, trace each child's hand and put a piece of yarn long enough to make a necklace through it. Print each child's name on one side!

Start the big day by taking everyone's picture with an instant developing camera. Pin these up and let children find "themselves" and label each with their name—the names should be preprinted on small index cards. As an activity, cover the names and parts of the photo and have children guess who the person is. If you have a sheet handy, try covering up actual parts of the children's bodies and then, let other children try guessing who they are.

Give out the hand necklaces that you have made the day before. Discuss how everyone is special—one of a kind. Have children compare their handprints.

GAMES AND PROJECTS

After discussing the physical things that make us all different and belong only to us, try some of the following art activities.

Body Outlines

Sometimes viewing one's body outline can be surprising and enlightening. Children may realize how tall they are or how long their legs are. It gives them a chance to get a better perspective of how their bodies look to others.

Have children lay down on a section of paper at least as big as they are. Trace their outline with magic marker and then cut it out. Mark each body outline with the child's name. It is great if you can display all of the body outlines on a wall of your classroom. (If this takes too long and you feel that your children will lose interest, an alternative is to have the children simply lie down on the floor and trace their body outlines with various colors of chalk and label them with each child's name.)

Thumbprint Collage

Explain how everyone has a thumbprint unlike anyone elses. If you have a teaching assistant, compare your thumbprints to show children what you are talking about. A magnifying glass may be helpful.

Let children dip their thumbs into instant chocolate pudding and then press them onto a large piece of light colored paper.

Label each child's print with her name. The, let them lick the chocolate pudding off their fingers. This eliminates clean-up time, not to mention the fun it creates.

Guess Who

Discuss how your voice is part of what makes you special. Tape everyone's voice into a tape recorder. Try to get each person's voice individually and leave spaces in between the voices which will allow you to pause or stop the recorder while children try to guess whose voice they are hearing when you play the tape back.

Master of Disguises—Who am I?

Discuss how no matter what you put on your body—you are still you. Have available a "Bag of Disguises" to illustrate your point. Allow children to experiment with the disguises. Let them, one at a time, disguise themselves and have the others try to see through their disguises and guess who they are.

Some suggestions for your "Bag of Disguises" are: wigs, scarves, jewelry, ties, lipstick, jackets, old team–sports uniforms, hats—hard hat, firefighter's hat, cowboy hat, helmet, mailcarrier's hat, police officer's hat. Try using your dress-up clothes for disguises.

Follow the Foot and Hand Prints

Trace and cut out hands and feet. Place these around your classroom or play area and let children follow the path. Make the path as interesting as possible—up, over, under, around.

END YOUR CELEBRATION WITH MUSIC
- "I Like Myself" from *Everbody Cries Sometimes*
- "What Is Your Name" from *Learning Basic Skills Through Music*
- Sing the following to the tune of "Where is Thumbkin."
   This is *child's name* (sung twice)
   He/She is a little *girl/boy* (sung twice)
   Child's name is in our class (sung twice)
   Glad *he/she* is here. (sung twice)

BREAD MASKS

YOU'LL NEED:

 2 cups flour

 3 Tblsp. oil

 ½-1 cup lukewarm water

 cookie sheets

 4 8" aluminum pie plates

 ½ tsp. salt

paintbrush

 bowl

food coloring

metal table knife (ADULT USE ONLY)

WHAT TO DO:

1. Measure flour and salt in bowl. Add oil and rub it in until mixture resembles coarse oatmeal.

2. Add ½ cup water. Blend with fingers. Add more water, if needed to form a dough you can gather into a ball.

3. Knead 10 minutes. Divide dough into 4-6 balls. Roll each 8" in diameter.

4. Place on the flat bottom of an inverted pie plate.

5. Cut in features with a metal table knife. Pinch features in dough with fingers.

6. Form other features with pieces of dough. Attach dough to dough with water.

7. Place pie plates on cookie sheets. Bake in 350°F oven for 10-15 minutes. The masks can be painted with diluted food color.

8. Eat or display. **TO DISPLAY:** Place the painted mask in 250°F oven for 6-8 hours. Cool and then shellac.

CELEBRATE THE NEW SIBLING

KATHY FAGGELLA

During their preschool years, many of the children in your care will become siblings. This is definitely a time for celebration, but often the new brother or sister is NOT the one who is the center of attention. That job can fall to you, her teacher, and her classmates—another opportunity for fun and learning.

Shortly before a new sibling arrives, take a circletime to talk about babies and what they can and cannot do. Children often feel that new babies will immediately be playmates and thus are disappointed. Encourage others to talk about their expectations and experiences as older siblings. Read Everett Anderson's *Nine Month Long* by Lucille Clifton and *I Love My Baby Sister (Most of the Time)* by Elaine Edelman to explore feelings and expectations.

Have children bring in pictures of babies—themselves and siblings. If you can get several photos of the same child at different ages, you can use them to teach a lesson on sequence.

You may wish to help the new sibling make a special t-shirt to wear as soon as the baby is born. *You'll need:* a t-shirt, fabric crayons, paper, and an iron. Let the child draw a picture of herself doing something "grownup" on the paper with crayons. You write "I'm a Big Sister (Brother)" on the paper backwards. Follow the directions on the crayon box and iron the design onto the front of the t-shirt. You might ask parents to donate the t-shirts. Or as an alternative, you may wish to make one "New Brother" and one "New Sister" t-shirt at the beginning of the year to be worn by various members of the group at appropriate times. These can turn jealousy into pride!

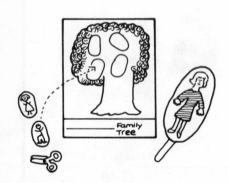

The arrival of a new baby is a good time to make simple family trees with your whole group. Have everyone draw a picture of each member of her family. Draw and duplicate an outline of a tree. Then, have children cut out each member's picture and glue it on the tree. The children will see how the new baby fits in the family and you will be able to judge and, if necessary, help the new sibling with her feelings about the situation.

You might suggest to parents that they send in lollipops or bags of raisins tied with pink or blue ribbons for their child to hand out to her classmates. Any opportunity you get, make the new sister or brother in your class feel special—and loved.

SOFT BABY

YOU'LL NEED:

1 stretch suit-zippered type is best

child's hat or cap

polyester stuffing

scissors

yarn (use child's hair color)

needle and thread

embroidery thread (use child's eye color)

 OR

old nylon stocking or polyester fabric

WHAT TO DO:

1. Sew arms of stretch suit closed. Sew up the snaps or zip up zipper. Stuff with polyester stuffing.

2. Cut out an 8" circle from stocking or fabric. Sew and gather edges to make a small bag-like shape. Stuff with polyester stuffing.

3. Use needle and thread to sew a soft sculpture face. Use embroidery thread to make eyes.

4. Sew on loops of yarn for hair.

5. Attach head securely to body with needle and thread.

6. Sew on hat or cap to head.

PROUD MOMENTS

KATHY FAGGELLA

Each small celebration can become a large learning opportunity for all the children. Read books like *Leo, the Late Bloomer* by Robert Krauss and *I Know a Lot of Things* by Ann and Paul Rand to inspire new accomplishments in your group. The following are a few suggestions for activities. Let them start you on your own ideas.

Shoe Tying

Let each child show off his new skill as he masters it. Glue a picture of a shoe onto a piece of cardboard. Punch holes the size shoelace holes would be. Reinforce holes with gummed reinforcements. Give the child a real piece of yarn for a lace. Wind transparent tape around each end and let him go in and out.

First Lost Tooth

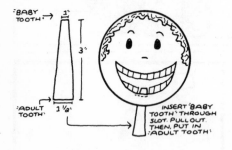

■ Make a face picture with a large grin, on a white paper plate. Cut a 1 ½″ slot where one missing tooth is. Cut a 3″ long strip of paper, 1″ at one end to 1 ½″ at the other. Place the 1″ end of the strip through the slot, so it looks like a baby tooth. Pull it out. Now, let the 1 ½″ end "grow" into place. Talk about care of loose teeth—how to eat and to brush, and about what happens as a new tooth grows in.

■ Put on a Toothy Play to show children how to brush teeth properly. Make a giant, life-sized set of teeth by dressing a group of children in white trash bags. Cut a slit for their heads and arms. Make a giant, cardboard toothbrush and let one child "brush" the teeth. Have one "tooth" fall out!

■ Read *One Morning in Maine* by Robert McClosky.

Build up your own library of books to be used for these special occasions. Read a story to the group as part of your "little celebration." For example, to celebrate the arrival of a new pet either in the classroom or at someone's home, you might read:
• *Angus and the Cat* by Marjorie Flack
• *Millions of Cats* by Wanda Gag
• *Whistle for Willie* by Ezra Jack Keats
• *Can I Keep Him?* by Steven Kellog
• *Birds and Fishes* by Brian Wildsmith

FISH BOWL PICTURES

YOU'LL NEED:

 chunks of parafin wax

 white paper

 tape

 paintbrush

scissors

cotton tip stick

 black paper

plastic kitchen wrap

 blue food color-diluted with water

WHAT TO DO:

1.
Draw fish shapes on white paper with parafin wax chunks. (Shapes will be almost invisible.)

2.
Using a cotton tip stick or paintbrush, wash diluted food color over entire paper. Let dry thoroughly.

3.
Frame painting by cutting out a fish bowl shape in middle of black paper.

4.
On the back, tape down a piece of plastic kitchen wrap. From the front, the page will look like a glass fishbowl.

5.
Finally, tape fish painting to back of black paper so fish appear to be swimming in the "bowl."

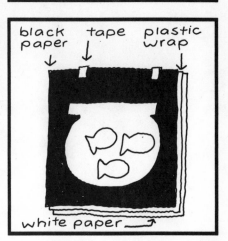
black paper   tape   plastic wrap

white paper

BIRTHDAYS IN SCHOOL

FRANCINE JARONCYZK

The passing of a year. Three hundred and sixty five days of discoveries, adventures, new relationships, and growth—a triumph to be celebrated with friends and loved ones. How do we handle children's birthdays during the school year?

One method is to celebrate once a month. The teacher and/or the children choose a day at the end of each month on which they celebrate all the birthdays that have passed during the month.

An alternative is to celebrate each child's individual birthdate with acccommodations made for those birthdates that fall on days when there is no school.

There are many arguments for and against each of these methods. The once-a-month celebration takes less time away from other activities, may cost less (if party supplies have to be purchased), makes celebrations less personal, and therefore may focus less attention on the financial circumstances of each child's family. The individual method gives each and every child special attention, lets no one's birthdate pass unnoticed, and adds many more joyous festivities to our calendars. (Can you guess which method I prefer?)

ORGANIZATION TIPS

If you have decided on the monthly collective celebration, write the names of everyone who has a birthday next to the name of the month on the calendar. Highlight the day you have chosen for the celebration.

If you are celebrating each child's birthday individually, mark the special days each month on your class calendar. Write the child's name on the date and draw a birthday cake or balloon around it to make it easy to locate birthdays and count how many fall in each month.

TREATS

Give out treats in individual baskets or bags clearly marked with each child's name (one extra for emergencies). These should be prepared before the party by the teacher or parents.

This method works better than passing around large baskets or plates of goodies. It allows you to control the amount of goodies each child consumes and it makes sure everyone gets an equal amount and no one is left out.

Good-for-you treats include: raisins, popcorn, apples, grapes, celery stuffed with cream cheese or peanut butter, cheese squares, dried fruit, and apple slices sprinkled with cinnamon or spread with peanut butter.

If you are asking parents to supply party treats, you can avoid doubles by having them list their name and contribution on a sheet beforehand. If you are trying to guide parent donations, provide a list of items you desire for the party and have them choose from given suggestions what they will contribute.

Give parents a deadline of at least one or two days before the party by which to bring in the goodies. This will give you time to fill in where they may have fallen short. It also eliminates perishable treats for which you may not have refrigeration available. Remember to give parents the exact number of children in your group, plus one for emergencies.

DECORATIONS

To make placemats, write each child's name on a fingerpainting and cover with clear contact paper. These can be used over and over again.

Make a crown for the birthday child out of construction paper if you are having individual celebrations. Decorate it with fake gems from broken costume jewelry. Have children make party hats by drawing pictures on construction paper. Roll paper into a cone shape and staple closed. Staple a string to each side to make a chin strap.

Make an ordinary chair into a throne for the day! With the children or by yourself, decorate a pillowcase with markers and stuff with an old pillow to place on the seat. Wrap crepe paper streamers around the chair's legs and arms.

Use children's art projects whenever possible to decorate. By using their art, you are showing them how valuable their creations are and they will feel more a part of the celebration.

ACTIVITIES

Have a **Sing-along.** Even the very shy do not mind belting out a song if they are one of twenty singers. Try to tape your group's favorites, silly songs, and old standbyes to get things started.

Play **Circle Blow**. Cut out three circles from construction paper and crease them in the middle. Tape a finish line on the floor. Have the children three at a time kneel down and try to blow the circles across the finish line.

Play **Bowling for Hats**. Place a few party hats on the floor and let the children try to knock the hats down by rolling a soft ball at them.

In general, play some games with one winner and others where everyone is a winner so no one goes home empty-handed.

BIRTHDAY BOARD

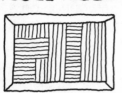

WHAT TO DO:

1. Cut posterboard or oaktag in 12 squares (1 for each month of the year) to fit size of bulletin board.

2. Mount each calendar page onto cardboard box, so it sets away from back of bulletin board. Attach each box to bulletin board.

3. With help of an adult, each child writes his name and birthdate on a clip style clothespin and clips it onto the appropriate calendar page.

4. Clip clothespins with a candle drawn on each to a posterboard birthday cake for celebrations.

5.   Add more clothespins to calendar bulletin board for field trips and special events.

PLAY A GAME-

Remove clip clothespins and see if children can guess their birthmonths. Then, reclip the clothespins

MAKE A GRAPH-

Label a long piece of paper with 12 months. Let children attach their clothespins to their birthmonths. Tally all January, February birthdays...

CELEBRATIONS FOR LEARNING

CREATE A HOLIDAY

Just as we might prepare a child for a hospital stay by role-playing the experience with her, we also can prepare our children for the "big" holidays by allowing them the freedom to invent, explore, and experiment with their own joyous celebrations. During a discussion about holidays, one group of preschoolers came up with a wonderful list of things they would like to celebrate as a holiday. We talked about "things we appreciate (are glad about)," "things that are special to us," "things we are proud of," and "things that are so wonderful that they ought to be celebrated." Their ideas included: ice cream, friends, and snow, and such accomplishments as: getting dressed by myself and growing big enough to reach the light switch.

The children chose "Pet Day" as their first "Do-It-Yourself Holiday." Together, we came up with the following plans and activities for their celebration.

ART ACTIVITIES
■ We made a collage of pet pictures. We cut out and collected them from old magazines. Later, we added a sign that said, "We Love Carrot"—our rabbit—and put it out on our front window like a flag on our special day.
■ We made "Pet Day cards"—a lot like a birthday card—to exchange with someone else as on Valentine's Day.
■ We made "Pet costumes." We decorated paper bags that fit over the children's bodies. The children wanted to "dress up as on Halloween and have a parade as on the Fourth of July."

FIELD TRIPS
■ We visited the pet shop to see what kinds of pets there were.
■ We visited the library to find pictures, records, and books about pets.

MUSIC/MOVEMENT ACTIVITIES
■ We explored how different pets move, how they act when they feel hungry, lonely, angry, frisky, tired...and how they "talk" to one another—all to music.

LANGUAGE DEVELOPMENT
■ We told, wrote, illustrated, and/or taperecorded a story about our favorite pets.
■ We made a "Be Nice to Your Pet" chart. We kept adding to it for the next several weeks.
■ We played Invent-a-Pet. We took the parts and characteristics we liked best from each favorite pet, and put them all together

How I Was Nice to My Pet

Bobby G.- "I brushed Spot's fur."
Sabrina - "I gave my cat a new toy."
Jason - "I took Sparky for a walk."

to describe a new pet. The children described an animal the size of a small pony, who had soft fur, long ears, and a short tail like a rabbit, purrs when you pat it, eats carrots, milk, and dog food, and barks like a dog (but not too loud). The children decided it would be blue and orange and called it a "Rabdat" (a rabbit-dog-cat)!

SNACKTIME
■ Have a "Pet Day Carrot Cake." and sing "Happy Pet Day to Us..." just like the Happy Birthday song.

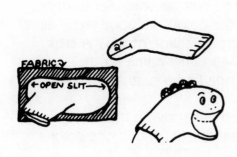

The special activities were spread out over a week leading up to our "holiday," two fitting into our regular routine each day. The atmosphere remained secure, supportive, and relaxed, and we avoided overdoing it. We saved the parade, hanging out our decorated "We Love Carrot" sign, the exchange of "Pet Day Cards," and our snack celebration for the holiday itself.

As it turned out, "Pet Day" lasted a long time. The children continued to play with handmade puppets and pet costumes throughout the following week. Pets enjoyed more understanding and recognition, and children learned to celebrate with pure pleasure the value of their pets.

When we encourage children to enjoy and celebrate the goodness and the value of the simple things in life—as children do so often on their own—the message they receive is that all celebrations—even the "big," traditional holidays—are built around a simple idea.

PAPER BAG ANIMALS ON PARADE

HAVE A COLOR PARTY!

MARY BETH SPANN

Consider organizing a party with a single color in mind. Party games, food, poetry, and songs must all revolve around the chosen theme, and the children can wear clothes of the special color.

Aside from helping to involve them personally, the variety of shades that children will display in their clothing will make the dress-up element an important one in your party plans.

■ Try a discussion involving shade comparisons. For example: "We are all wearing red, but do the colors all look exactly alike? Is anyone wearing a very light or pale shade of red? A dark shade of red? Does anyone know another name for this shade of red? (rose, burgundy...) Can anyone find a partner who is wearing the same shade as you are?"

From such a discussion, children will grow in their awareness of the similarities and differences that exist within one color range.

■ While enjoying a red snack (apples or strawberries, perhaps?), take advantage of the colorful treats by making up comparisons which may be recorded to create a group poem. "Apples are redder than _____, But not as red as _____ (sunset, a fire engine)."

■ Rhyming word games are great for getting the creative language juices flowing—how many words can you rhyme with *red*? After you think up your own list, ask the same question to your children. Encourage both real and ridiculous answers.

■ Don't overlook paint strips—available in paint and hardware stores—as free materials for instant playing fun. Each strip provides a variety of tints belonging to the same color family, and each tint is usually labeled with a "colorful" name for easy identification. Challenge children to correctly identify "Radish Red" or "Tomato Surprise;" then, let them make up their own titles.

Cutting the strips apart offers another approach. Scramble the individual chips, and ask children to match identical pairs or put the shades in order from darkest to lightest. If they are able to do so, ask them to tell you how they solved the puzzle.

■ A familiar story will seem extra-special, when presented during the color celebration. "Little Red Riding Hood" or "The Little Red Hen" would be good choices for rounding out a red theme.

To make sure that the fun and learning will last, create a display with colorful, interesting objects that carry out the color theme.

A TEDDY BEAR TEA

MARY BETH SPANN

Fun and learning go hand in hand when stuffed animals are invited to a party. When your children hear the news—that their teddy bears are being invited to spend the day in school—they will be excited.

Any successful party needs careful planning, and children will be more than eager to help organize this creative adventure. To inform the parents of your plans, have each child cut out and decorate a large, bear-shaped card on which they will paste a preprinted invitation.

Tea, honey, and sugar cookies are the perfect tea party menu, so the next step is to get together the necessary supplies: ingredients for the cookie dough, aluminum foil, raisins, tea bags, honey, tea cups, and a teapot.

The day before the party, children shape dough in bear-shaped cookies by rolling their dough into three small balls and flattening the balls to create two round ears and a head. They decorate these with raisin eyes and noses for a delicious finishing touch.

Children work their dough on prelabeled squares of foil which can be easily transferred to cookie sheets for baking. When it is time to distribute the goodies, it's a snap to match the labeled cookie with its delighted baker. Names may be attached to the foil with masking tape, or the names may be printed directly on the foil before baking.

During circletime, everyone has an opportunity to introduce their guest, and to tell the group how the bear came to live with them. The various shapes and sizes of the bears provide an interesting math lesson—to try to sort and classify the furry friends.

The honey-laced tea and bear-shaped cookies are delicious, even to the bears! For a special touch, use honest-to-goodness china tea cups and saucers; children will be on their best—and most careful—manners.

Following the refreshments, perform some teddy bear fingerplays and poems. Sing some songs such as: "The Bear Went Over the Mountain," and "Teddy Bear Picnic," then, listen to a bear story like "Goldilocks and the Three Bears."

End the festivities with an exciting game to match the theme of the day. On a large piece of brown craft paper, draw a simple outline of a teddy bear with marking pens. Use a blindfold and paper bowties to play "Pin the Tie on the Teddy."

AND IN THE CENTER RING...

FRANCINE JARONCYZK

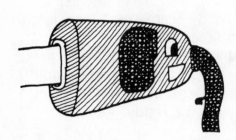

Many children visit the circus or at least watch TV commercials for it. Capitalize on their interest and celebrate the circus. Take your group behind the scenes and create a puppet circus! Homemade clowns and dancing elephants can do anything their creators wish—sing, dance, walk a tightrope.

This type of performance does not require memorizing prewritten lines or scenes. It does provide an opportunity for even the shy to hide behind the puppet character they are manipulating and to be bold, silly, loud, ferocious, or daring.

It also requires a certain amount of preparation and committment. The degree of attention to details, the size and makeup of your audience, and the selection of each type of puppet's performance can all be decided by your group.

To help your young performers decide in which way they want to contribute, provide research materials such as: old circus programs, filmstrips, and library books—*Careers with the Circus* by Karen Kelly: *Circus* by Beatrice Schenk de Regniers, *Circus* by Brian Wildsmith. After all, their hearts may be set on making acrobat puppets, but they may not be sure what an acrobat does!

After allowing time for research and a reasonable time for each child to change his mind at least a half dozen times, make a class chart—perhaps a picture chart—listing each child's name and his final choice. This may be the time to also decide what each child's puppet will do. However, it is sometimes necessary for children to work with their puppets before they can really decide what their performance will be.

You may be wondering if a chart is really necessary. I think so because it forces the children to make a choice and stick to it—a type of committment. This particular project may take as long as two weeks to complete, so you may understand my strong suggestion that you obtain a committment from the children.

For those who show no interest in committing themselves to the art of puppet-making, do not despair! Try to enlist their help in: constructing the tent, making a program, distributing tickets, or perhaps being the ring master.

Once you have made the puppets, just add some props, a tent, and a tightrope, and you've got it! What the children decide to do with these puppets should be entirely up to them. Some children need no encouragement to spark their imagination and others need suggestions and guidance. Provide poems, background music, simple songs, and let the little performers take over.

The benefits of such an activity are many, but to me the self-esteem and pride gained from a cheering audience will make any project of this size well worth the effort.

CLOWN PARTY

1. PAPER PLATE CLOWN

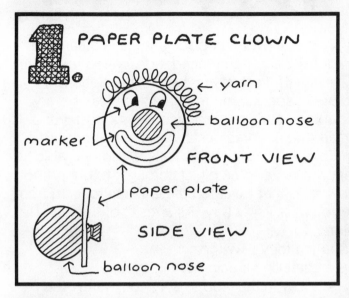

yarn

balloon nose

marker

FRONT VIEW

paper plate

SIDE VIEW

balloon nose

2. CLOWN POSTER

CLOWNS

Use colored construction paper and wet, colored chalk.

3. CLOWN MAKE-UP

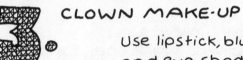

Use lipstick, blush-on, and eye shadow applied with clean cotton swabs or make GREASE PAINT:

2 Tblsp. white shortening

2 Tblsp. cornstarch

1 tsp. flour

Color with cocoa or food colors.

4. CLOWN TRAIN

Make a train from large boxes and paper plates.

5. CLOWN SANDWICHES

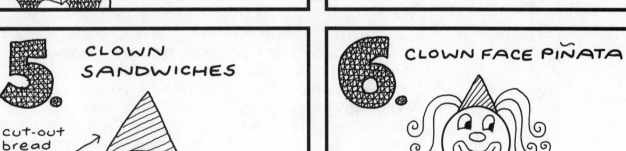

cut-out bread slices spread with peanut butter

raisins

strawberry jelly

raisins

shredded coconut

6. CLOWN FACE PIÑATA

Cover a large balloon with strips of newspaper dipped into a thick mixture of wallpaper paste and water. Let dry. Glue on tissue paper hair and paint on a face. Pop the balloon. Fill with candy and toys

MISS PIGGY DAY

ELLEN JAVERNICK

Perky Miss Piggy is wallowing in popularity, so I planned a Miss Piggy Day for my class. Beforehand, I decorated the room with Miss Piggy materials. Posters are available in stationery shops, but I ordered a special one from the American Library Association. For about $6.00, we received a large poster and 300 matching bookmarks. Your librarian can order some for you. Since we live in Colorado, a pig-raising state, I also was able to arrange in advance to have some piglets brought to our school.

I selected a few facts that I wanted the children to learn from their experiences on Miss Piggy Day. As a result of the day, I wanted the children to:
• Recognize pigs when they saw them
• Know that pigs are intelligent animals
• Know that pigs wallow in the mud to stay cool, rather than because they are dirty animals

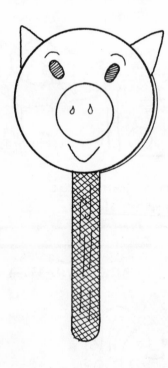

MISS PIGGY PUPPET

Within the room. I set up the following areas:
■ At the art table, we made Miss Piggy Puppets. For each puppet, you will need one sheet of 8½" by 11" pink construction paper and one popsicle stick. Older children can trace twice around a 5½"-circle and once around a 2"-circle. With younger children, you can have the circles drawn, or, if necessary, even cut. Have the children assemble the pig puppets by gluing the stick between the two large circles; then, adding the smaller circle for a snout. Let children cut ears from the pink scraps and glue them on. Have them use black crayon to draw eyes.
■ In the science area, we experimented with "mud." Before the children came to this area, I prepared it in the following way. First, I covered the floor with an old worktable cover. I taped it down, so it would not slip. Next, I covered the area with newspaper. I set out a 9" by 13" pan filled with fairly thick "mud"—brown paint. Between that tray and another tray of warm soapy water, I placed a pile of inexpensive drawing paper. When children came to the science center, they took off their shoes and socks. One at a time, they stepped into the mud. While they were standing there, I asked questions like, "How does it feel?", "Do you think you would like to lay down in it?", "Do you think that pigs would stay cool if they were lying in the mud?" (Actually, this is the real reason that pigs need to have mud to wallow in— they do not perspire, so they must keep their skin cool and damp.) After each child had a chance to wiggle his toes in the mud, I showed him a picture of a pig's hoof. Then, the child stepped out onto the drawing paper and

made a print of his foot.

Finally, he stepped into the warm soapy water and washed his feet. We did not put our shoes back on until circletime, so we checked carefully to see that feet were clean and dry before children moved from this area.

■ In our housekeeping area, we put out a variety of pig products. We stocked our refrigerator and cupboard shelves with empty containers of sausage, bacon, and so on.

■ In one corner of the room, we set up a barn and a variety of farm animals. We talked about the differences in animals, encouraging them to recognize similarities and differences.

■ At one of our worktables, I set out a balance scale with a variety of objects with pig pictures taped to them. Children worked to find out which was the heaviest pig.

■ Have a pigathalon (If the weather is nice, you could set this up outside.) Begin by taping the course on the floor. Set up a tube or box for a tunnel, a feed trough filled with "corn" (styrofoam pellets), a shed to sleep in, and so on.

Before a child begins the pigathalon, stuff a pillow in his shirt. Then, ask him to crawl through the course with his fat tummy dragging. Have him wiggle his nose in the 'corn,' rest for a count of 10 in the shed, and so on. As in a marathon, the victory is in completing the race. Everyone is a winner!

■ With children's shoes still off, play "This Little Pig Went to the Market."

■ Dramatize the story of the Three Little Pigs. Sing "Who's Afraid of the Big Bad Wolf?" Ask questions to get at the idea that the third little pig was smart. Follow up with some facts about real pigs' intelligence.

■ If you serve snacks, you may want to make pig sandwiches. Spread one large bread circle with cream cheese—colored pink. Top each with a smaller pink snout. Use raisins for eyes and the bread scraps for ears. If you have time, children easily can prepare the snack themselves.

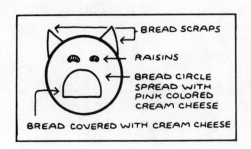

BREAD SCRAPS

RAISINS

BREAD CIRCLE SPREAD WITH PINK COLORED CREAM CHEESE

BREAD COVERED WITH CREAM CHEESE

At the end of the morning, I handed out "Hogs are Beautiful" buttons. We received these free through our local hog farmers' association. Miss Piggy would be glad to know she was the inspiration for such a fun-filled, learning experience.

OUTER SPACE PARTY

KATHY FAGGELLA

Nothing stands for our technical achievements and our greatest fantasies-come-true quite like our space flights. Children will enjoy preparing for and having a "Space" Party.

UFOs

Slow and constant motion seem to characterize activity in space. These homemade UFOs will add this quality to your setting.

You'll Need:
- 8 flat magnets (not horseshoe)
- large cardboard box
- thread
- 4 empty small pill botles, jewel boxes, or other small lightweight containers
- 4 empty salt boxes, jars

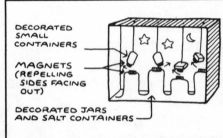

DECORATED SMALL CONTAINERS

MAGNETS (REPELLING SIDES FACING OUT)

DECORATED JARS AND SALT CONTAINERS

What to Do:
1. Arrange the magnets in pairs so that the sides that repel each other are facing. Mark each repelling side.
2. Now, glue a magnet to the bottoms of each of the small containers. Make sure the repelling side faces out.
3. Glue the other four magnets to the tops of the empty salt boxes and jars. Glue boxes and jars to cardboard box bottom.
4. Attach thread to small containers by opening lid, and then gluing closed.
5. Attach other end of thread to box top. The magnets should be very close, but not touching.
6. Decorate containers and cover bottom ones with fabric.

Space Docking Game

Tie string to four corners of a piece of cardboard (about 2' x 2'). Gather the four ends of the strings and knot. Attach knot to ceiling or doorsill. The "space station" should hang about one foot over children's heads. Now, have children fly paper airships onto platform.

CREATIVE MOVEMENT

Creative movement gives children the opportunity not only to move and develop their bodies, but also to become aware of what their bodies can do and how they move in their own personal space.

The Launch:

Children squat down. Begin a countdown at 10. At 3- 2-1- "blast off" children jump up high—great for concentration.

In Space:

Have children walk around in slow motion with large strides to simulate the weightless feeling of astronauts. Add balloons for children to gently toss and catch.

The EVA:
(extravehicular activity)

A space walk is fun for children. Cut 6-8 pieces of waistband elastic each six feet long. Tie each around a child's waist and the other ends to a chair. Sit on the chair and have children s-t-r-e-t-c-h out and around in slow motion. Use soft music to accompany this space walk.

SPACE PARTY

Paint a large corner mural bright blue with many stars.

Hang a large mobile by attaching cardboard cut-out moon and star shapes with yarn to long dowels. Cover cardboard with aluminum foil and silver glitter.

Paint a refrigerator carton to resemble a rocket. Add a paper cone to the top and red and orange streamers to the bottom (the hot exhaust, of course). Cut an arched doorway and round porthole. Cover porthole with cellophane.

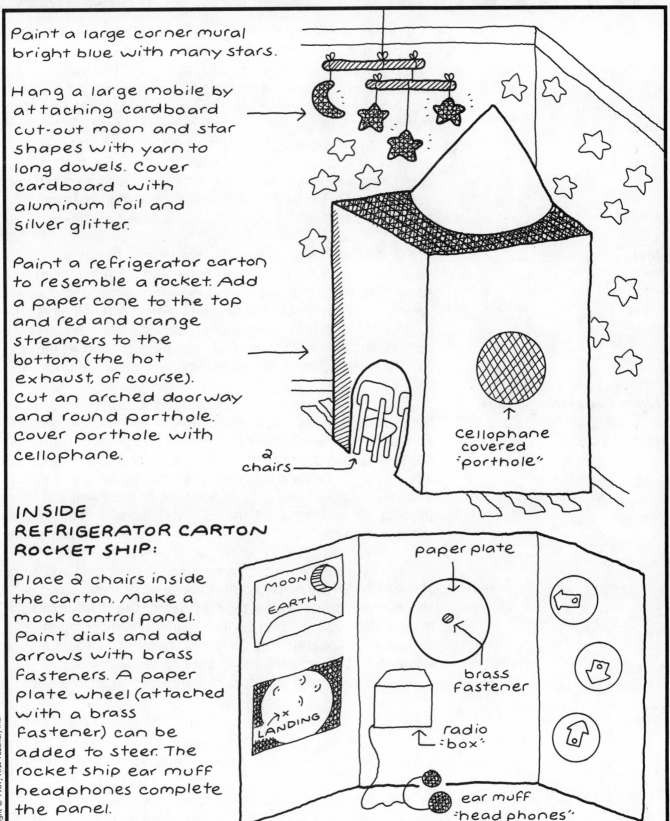

cellophane covered "porthole"

2 chairs

INSIDE REFRIGERATOR CARTON ROCKET SHIP:

Place 2 chairs inside the carton. Make a mock control panel. Paint dials and add arrows with brass fasteners. A paper plate wheel (attached with a brass fastener) can be added to steer. The rocket ship ear muff headphones complete the panel.

MOON
EARTH

LANDING

paper plate

brass fastener

radio "box"

ear muff "head phones"

95

CELEBRATE MY FAMILY

FRANCINE JARONCYZK

There are many types of families today. Some involve only one parent, some stepparents and siblings, and a few have live-in grandparents. It is extremely important that we make our children feel comfortable and secure with the particular "family" that they have. They also need to have an understanding of the fact that families change for many different reasons: birth, death, divorce, marriage, adoption, and so on.

Together with your children, plan a "Family Celebration." It could be a weeklong event with different activities each day or you can center the whole celebration around one of the suggestions that follow.

Dress Up Like _____

Ask the children to choose one family member they want to be like someday. Have them go home and ask that person for some clothing or other personal belongings which the child will wear or bring to school the next day. Each child will have time to tell the group something about that person which makes them so special. Have a tea party (milk and cookies) and let the children pretend they are whomever they are dressed up as.

Family Gettogether in Class

Invite special family members to share something of themselves with the class. Together with the children, prepare special invitations to be sent home—drawings on construction paper folded into a note from you. Tell parents about your intention to "celebrate the children's families" on a given date and time. Explain briefly the importance of this event and invite them to join in. Give a definite RSVP date and leave a space on the invitation for family members to write in any special talents, hobbies, and so on, they would be willing to share with the group. Make sure you specify the time—a beginning and an end. This will hopefully help parents choose what they would like to share—you cannot build a model boat for the children in 10 minutes, but you can bring one in that is already completed.

Keep a reminder notice in a highly visible place for at least a week so that no one will forget the big day.

Help children prepare some refreshments for their families.

ACTIVITIES

■ Allow children to bring in family photo albums to share with the class. Afterward, help them illustrate family stories while you fill in the text.

■ Make paper dolls of men, women, boys, girls, and pets. Allow children to select the appropriate dolls that represent their family members, draw features on them and glue them inside a shallow cardboard box (or lid) labeled "This Is My Family" with the child's name.

■ Take candid shots of family members coming in the morning, helping with hats and coats, kissing and hugging their child, smiling and laughing with the child, coming to visit with the class, returning to pick their child up. Display these pictures on a bulletin board or a poster and let the children talk about their family member or members. Watch their pride as they spot their special someone(s).

■ Provide lots of props and clothes in your dramatic play area to help children act out family scenes.

■ Include books in your library area like:
• *Daddy* by Jeannette Caines
• *Big Sister, Little Sister* by Charlotte Zolotow
• *Grandpa* by Barbara Borack
• *Grownups Cry Too* by Nancy Hazen
• *A Look at Death* by Rebecca Anders

■ Play music like "Parents Are People" from *Free to Be Me*.

Above all, show all your children that each and every family is special—and perfect for them.

A FAMILY TREE

YOU'LL NEED:

small tree branch - 1 per child

juice can - 1 per child

tape

glue

sand or plaster of Paris

small pieces of typing (or manilla paper)

construction paper

crayons, felt tip pens, or colored pencils

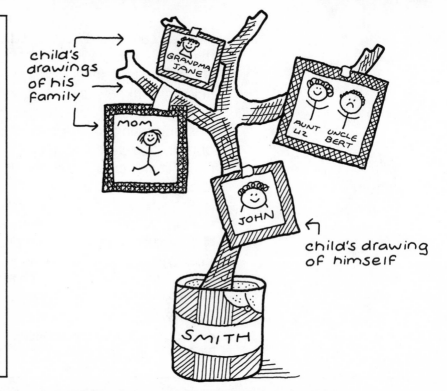

child's drawings of his family

child's drawing of himself

WHAT TO DO:

1. Have each child make drawings of his family. (Make sure the child includes significant people in his life - uncles, aunts, grandparents.)

2. Label each drawing as the child tells you.

3. Mount drawings on construction paper.

4. Set branch into juice can with sand or plaster of Paris.

5. Have child tape drawings onto branches with a drawing of himself taped to the "main branch."

6. Write child's surname (last name) on a strip of paper. Tape onto juice can. Discuss how families include young or older people.

MULTICULTURAL CELEBRATIONS

CELEBRATE AROUND THE WORLD

MARTHA A. HAYES

Children all over the world are alike in many ways. One special similarity is their enjoyment of celebrations—often called feast days. These are times when families gather together, serve special food, observe certain customs, and take time to think of others or of the good things that have happened to the family.

Many of the celebrations began a part of a religious observance, and some continue to be observed as part of the Church calendar. Others have become more secular, but still take place. Other festivities take place to honor a particular event in history, such as Bastille Day in France.

Some celebrations were started to honor a needed weather or calendar change. In Brazil, for instance, one Indian tribe has a ceremonial rain dance. The participants wear masks—one particular kind represents male and female fish. Iran's New Year's Day is the first day of spring: the total celebration lasts for 12 days. A month of preparation precedes it. It includes housecleaning and having children blanch almonds for a candied treat. The New Year's Day dinner must have seven foods whose name begins with S.

Japan seems to have more special days just for children. The boy's festival, which now has been expanded to include girls, is celebrated on May 5. The importance of being good, strong, courageous citizens is stressed. Doll festivals take place on March 3 in Japan. Collections of dolls are displayed and families come to visit and see each other's sets.

On New Year's Day in Japan, everybody has a birthday; homes are decorated and greeting cards are sent. Boys and girls buy paper fortunes and tie them to the branches of trees in the hope that this will bring the one who ties it on good luck.

Chinese New Year takes place in mid-winter, with young and old dressing up, parading, shooting off firecrackers, and taking part in all types of fun.

Did you know that April Fool's Day started in France when the Pope changed the calendar so that the year started, not in April, but in January? The fools were the ones who couldn't remember the right date. People used to stuff paper fish down one another's shirts.

Ask children to tell about special days that they celebrate in their homes. You can celebrate them in your classroom, too.

Obviously, it is not suggested that you celebrate every holiday. But, a celebration at a low time in the year can be just the thing to lift spirits and get things moving again.

CELEBRATE! CELEBRATE!

JEANNINE PEREZ

I began teaching multicultural units as units on each country or region, emphasizing holidays. This worked fairly well, but I found that children under six remember mainly what they've made, sung, or eaten, so the concept of geography and individual countries is lost.

Now, my biggest emphasis in multicultural education is celebrating the differences in various cultures. It amazes children, at first, that there are thousands of different cultures, and that they all work pretty well! By celebrating the differences, we learn to appreciate and respect them.

BASIC ACTIVITIES AND HINTS

■ To encourage simple map skills, I start early in the year with activities and bulletin boards, centering on WHERE I LIVE...PICTURES OF THE HOUSE I LIVE IN...THE BLOCK OR AREA AROUND ME.

■ I use all the resource people I can locate. I am lucky to have parents coming from South Africa, Korea, Iran, and China, who are delighted to cook a snack, show pictures, wear costumes, or teach songs in their native language. If these people were not available, I would consult the phone book for ethnic restaurants, groceries, or university programs, or foreign exchange students, who could share with the children.

■ The globe is handy for daily use, whether while discussing projects, foods, or places in the news, or even to locate the origin of fairy tales or settings for stories we read. Children can become familiar and comfortable with global concepts.

■ There are many books on the preschool level with settings in far-off lands, and children love to hear them. Take time to discuss and share afterwards. Your librarian can help you find good books. Here are some of our favorites:
- *Anansi, the Spider* by Gerald McDermott
- *Ootah's Lucky Day* by Peggy Parish
- *Gilberto and the Wind* by Marie Ets
- *Mexicali Soup* by Kathryn Hitte and William Haynes
- *Tikki Tikki Tembo* by Arlene Mosel
- *Pancho* by Berta and Elmer Hader
- *Bringing the Rain to Kapiti* by Verna Aardema

■ A big wall map gives a different perspective than a globe. A younger child is limited in experience and knowledge, is egocentric, and wants activities centered around himself. By widening his world, you help him begin to consider others and how his actions affect others.

■ Simply learning "Hello" in as many languages as possible, becomes a game, and more than a game.

MUSIC PROJECTS

Music and art go hand in hand with celebrations, especially in different cultures. Musical instruments can be made of almost anything that produces a sound. It would be good to find pictures of different instruments, and listen to records of music from different cultures before experimenting with your own. Ella Jenkins' *Rhythms of Childhood African Impressions* is a good start with simple melodies and rhythms. Some instrument projects might include:

■ Making drums from oatmeal boxes, upside-down plastic baskets, or ice cream containers

■ Making rattles from juice cans, baking powder cans, or coffee cans with pebbles, beans, metal nails, or screws. Experiment with the different sound each makes.

■ Using a long stick to do a Limbo Dance, with two children holding it lower and lower, as a child attempts to go under without touching it. The other children can clap a rhythm.

■ Making an African bongo drum from a large coffee can with parts of a rubber inner-tube, as the top.

■ Making a wooden xylophone, a long-term project, using 8½" x 2" boards or bamboo poles, cut 12" and shorter. Place on a strip of carpet and strike with a wooden mallet or stick. Children can help measure, sand, saw, and varnish the parts.

■ Doing the Mexican Hat Dance, a simplified version. Children join hands in a large circle. Everyone dances to the right (one heel forward, then alternate feet), until the music changes; then everyone turns and dances to the left, (one heel forward, then alternate feet). Dance to the center of the circle, with hands held high; dance back, bending low.

Any Mexican music can be used; but the Hat Dance Song is best! Children may want to make a guitar from a foil pie pan nailed to a 3' x 2' board with rubber bands stretched across it.

ART PROJECTS

There are as many multicultural art projects as anyone would wish; however, some are ready-made for the joy of celebrating cultural holidays and lifestyles.

■ Oriental tissue paper flowers, made from accordian-folded pieces of bright tissue paper, caught in the center with pipecleaners and spread into huge blooms, make any center bright and gay.

■ Oriental lanterns from wallpaper samples or heavy paper are quick to make.

■ Totem poles can be made from wood scraps or from cardboard tubes, decorated, then glued together.

ORIENTAL LANTERN

SPECIAL CELEBRATIONS

Here are some special days that we celebrate at our center.

■ By celebrating Rosh Hashanna, the Jewish New Year, we learn many new vocabulary words—*shofar*, the ram's horn which is blown, (children love to simulate this) and *challah*, a bread shaped like a ladder (people go up or down in the world; their choice). We use a simple French Bread recipe, and let children help shape and eat it. We also eat apple wedges, dipped in honey.

■ The first day of spring is the Iranian New Year, *Nu Ruz*. *Nu Ruz* means "new life," and it is a celebration of the new life in spring. To help celebrate, we grow wheat or sprouts in a dish. We set the table with the greens, a bowl of goldfish, a mirror, eggs decorated in colors, candy, and breads. There is also a candle for each family member. Our resource person told us that the candle and plants signify new life; the seven foods starting with Iranian S—the goodness of Allah; the egg on the mirror—a superstition that the earth trembles on New Year's Day. She also advised us that on the 13th day of the New Year, it is unlucky to be indoors, which makes a perfect excuse to have snacks outside.

■ We have our own adaptation of Luilak, an obscure holiday celebrated in Holland. It falls on an early May Saturday. We use it whenever winter has become too long and too much!

Luilak means "lazybones," and on that special day, children in small towns join in groups and walk through the towns singing and making noise to wake up "Winter Lazybones" and make him disappear.

We get out the instruments, make silly hats, go outside all we can, or make a parade inside if we must, and for five minutes, make all the noise we can! Winter cannot dare stay much longer!

Limbo stick

RESOURCE BOOKS
• *About Us: The Childcraft Annual*
• *Resources for Creative Teaching in Early Childhood Education* by Bonnie Mack Flemming and Darlene Softley Hamilton
• *Children's Festivals from Many Lands* by Nina Miller
• *Customs and Holidays Around the World* by Lavinia Dobler
• *European Folk Festivals* by Sam and Beryl Epstein

By learning about the celebrations and customs in different cultures, children can learn to appreciate and respect differences in all people. Hopefully by doing this, we plant the seeds of respect for other lifestyles, curiosity about the places where customs originated, and openmindedness about people, dress, and foods that are unfamiliar.

TWO JAPANESE FESTIVALS

JANET HOROWITZ

THE MOON-VIEWING FESTIVAL

In Japan, the October moon is supposed to be the brightest full moon of the year, and the month of October is supposed to be the perfect month as far as the weather is concerned.

On the night of the full moon, hundreds of people walk into the country, or up a mountain, or to the seashore—anywhere where they can get a clear view of the moon.

As they go, everyone sings or whistles or plays the harmonica. When they arrive at their favorite moon-viewing place, they stand and admire the beauty before them. Children and adults often write poems about the moon.

As the family walks back home, they gather some of the wild grasses by the roadside. There are seven kinds of grasses called the "Seven Grasses of Autumn," and family members always try to gather some of each kind. They make them into floral arrangements, which they place in the home.

To celebrate the "Moon-Viewing" festival with your class, go on a picnic to an outdoor spot where there are wild flowers or fall leaves. The finding and sharing of the leaves or flowers is part of the lovely experience. If possible, have each child take her picnic lunch in a basket as the Japanese do.

Tell children how, in Japan, members of the group sometimes write short poems about the trees, flowers, and the moon to express their thanks and joy.

Your children may want to dictate their own poems or thoughts which they can illustrate later and take home.

DOLL FESTIVALS

Doll festivals are eagerly awaited by Japanese children, as they are the only times during the year that the family's old dolls are unpacked for display and doll stories are told.

Prepare now for a classroom doll festival (early in March).

- Have each child make her own doll.
- Plan a party. Make doll invitations and invite parents and friends to visit and admire the new dolls.
- Have a doll-naming ceremony.
- Let children take their dolls home throughout the year and bring them back for visits. Share "doll stories" at special circletimes. "Last night my doll slept at Grandma's with me."

ROLY POLY DOLLS

YOU'LL NEED:

 yarn—for hair

pebble

 glue

permanent markers

plastic egg-shaped hosiery container

- OR -

real egg with insides taken out (Have ½" hole at "pointed" top and shake out yolk and white).

WHAT TO DO:

1. Open the plastic container and glue pebble to the bottom — OR — IF using a real egg shell, glue pebble to bottom and cover hole with yarn hair.

(inside) pebble

½ plastic egg shell

yarn hair

egg shell

(inside) pebble

2. Decorate with markers in red and blue.

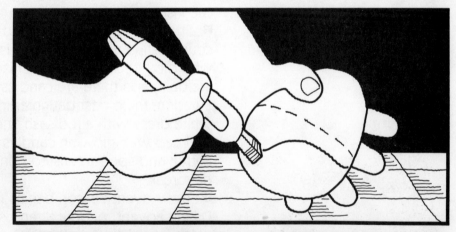

3. Push doll over — and it returns to a stable position.

FESTIVALS OF LIGHT

CYNTHIA BARNETT

One of the major goals of the Columbus Magnet school is to teach students to understand and appreciate the differences in others. The Festival of Lights was one of the celebrations in which this goal was realized. Because of the positive response, we wanted to share our success with you, in hopes that you might want to create a Festival of Lights celebration at your learning center.

The goal of the Festival of Lights was to show students and parents how lights are used in celebrations in different cultures. We selected celebrations that would reflect the school population. We used a large open space to set up tables for display. The traditions represented were:

■ Divali (Dee-Wah—lee) which is celebrated in India and is one of the most exciting holidays for children. It is celebrated in early November or late October. Garlands of flowers are hung over outside doors and good luck symbols are drawn on the doors with colored powders. Diyas—little clay saucers—are lit and placed on the window sills, on roofs, and along the roads. This is done to attract the goddess Lakshmi, a Hindu goddess, who, the Indians believe, will bring them wealth and good fortune, if she visits their homes.

■ St. Lucia's Day is celebrated on December 13 by many countries in Europe. This day is celebrated to honor St. Lucia, who died because of her Christian beliefs. In Italy, large bonfires are built, and there are candles and torchlight processions. In Sweden, the oldest daughter in the family dresses up in a long white dress with a red sash and places a crown of evergreens adorned with glowing candles on her head. It is her task to serve coffee and special twisted buns with raisins to her family at daybreak.

■ The Advent Season begins four Sundays before Christmas. During advent, people attend special church services and make plans for celebrating the birth of Jesus. Advent wreaths are made of evergreens and are placed flat on the dining tables in homes. Three purple candles and one pink candle are placed in the wreath. The candles are lighted each night. One purple candle is lit the first week of Advent, two the next week. On the third week, the pink candle is lit to signal that it is almost time for Christmas. One large white candle is placed in the center of the wreath. It is lit on Christmas day to represent the birth of Jesus. Christmas trees and calendars also are used in this celebration.

■ Kwanza is an Afro-American celebration. Kwanza means "first fruits." Celebration of harvesting the first fruits is traditional in Africa. Africans get together to give thanks for their blessings. Families sing, dance, and have a large Karamub (feast). It lasts seven days from December 26 to January 1. The Kinara is the special candleholder of the Kwanza celebration. The Kinara holds seven candles (usually red). One is lit each of the seven nights.

■ Los Posados means "lodging." It is celebrated in the USA by some Spanish Americans. The holiday begins on December 15. It is a reenactment of Joseph and Mary's trip from Nazareth to Bethlehem, seeking lodging the night before Jesus was born. It is celebrated by people going from house to house singing songs in English and Spanish, lighting their way with candles.

■ Hanukkah is a festival of lights observed by Jewish people. It celebrates the religious freedom for Jews. Candles are lit each night in a candleholder called a menorah. Families enjoy potato pancakes, called latkes. Children like to play games with a dreidel. Gifts are given to children, one each night. Hanukkah is celebrated usually in late November or early December.

We set up a schedule. At 20 minute intervals, a different class visited. Parent volunteers and their children explained how lights were used in each celebration. The students listened attentively and really enjoyed the three traditional foods that were offered: pieces of twisted buns from Sweden for St. Lucia Day; potato pancakes—Hanukkah; and sweets from India.

NEW YEAR'S AROUND THE WORLD

DR. MARGERY A. KRANYIK

"Happy New Year!" This greeting signifies the celebration of the first holiday of the year. To anyone who celebrates, it means a new beginning—a time to look ahead to the new year.

The new year is celebrated throughout the world. New Year's is an excellent holiday to explore because many ethnic groups involve their children directly in their traditions. As you discuss each country, use a globe to point out its location.

In Belgium, the day before New Year's is known as Sylvester's Day. The child who gets out of bed last is called "Sylvester" for the rest of the day. Children write letters telling of the good deeds they will do for their parents during the coming year. The letters are written on paper, decorated with fancy ribbons and flowers, and hidden away as a surprise. On New Year's Day, the children present the letters to their parents after breakfast and everyone goes to visit relatives.

Discuss the customs with your children. Help them make decorated letters telling about the good deeds they would like to do to give their parent and teachers.

The boys and girls in Bulgaria parade through the streets on New Year's Day carrying tree branches decorated with paper flowers. They knock on doors and rush in to tap each member of the family for good luck. They receive doughnuts called kolaches (kol a chees) and leave with the kolaches on their branches.

Have some small branches available for your children. After discussing the custom, decorate the branches with paper flowers, and have children go visiting neighbors or other classrooms.

In Greece, New Year's is known as St. Basil's Day, named after the saint who is known for his generosity and sympathy towards poor and unfortunate people. On the holiday, children carry miniatures of St. Basil's ship, accompanied by small drums and triangles. On the eve of St. Basil's Day, children collect their shoes and line them up in front of the fireplace before they go to bed. They believe that Saint Basil fills their shoes with toys and gifts. At midnight, the children are awakened to eat a piece of Saint Basil's cake, which has a coin baked in it. The first piece goes to the symbolic St. Basil, the next goes to the poor, the third piece to the oldest family member, the next to the adults. The last pieces are for the children. Whoever finds the coin in their piece will have good luck during the year.

Have a parade with ship replicas and rhythm instruments. Make your own Saint Basil's cake (Don't forget the penny!) and have the children act out the celebration.

These celebrations can be used throughout the winter months to learn about other cultures and have fun.

From the authors of
**CRAYONS
CRAFTS
AND
CONCEPTS**

CONCEPT COOKERY

by

Kathy Faggella

Through cooking experiences in the preschool classroom, children can develop basic skills and concepts. Organized by themes and concept areas, these 50+child and classroom tested recipes will fit naturally into your curriculum.

Easy-to-read, sequential recipe charts will appeal to your children as much as they do to you. Single page formats can easily be copied and sent home for parent follow up.

TABLE OF CONTENTS
- All about Me
- The Seasons
- Colors
- Shapes
- Language Development
- Children's Literature
- Celebrations and Holidays
- Science
- Opposites
- Math

TO ORDER:

Send $9.95 (plus $1 for each book's postage and handling) to:

First Teacher, Inc.
Box 29
60 Main St.
Bridgeport, CT. 06602

OR CALL: 1-800-341-1522

From the authors of
CONCEPT COOKERY

CRAYONS
CRAFTS
AND
CONCEPTS

by
Kathy Faggella

Art activities can teach basic concepts and be integrated into the whole curriculum. Presented in one page, easy-to-read formats, that even your children can follow, these 50+ projects will fit into each theme and subject area, you introduce. There are also suggestions for setting up an art area, making smocks, safety rules, and follow ups for each activity. Projects are designed to be reproduced and sent home for follow up, too.

TABLE OF CONTENTS

TO ORDER:

Send $9.95 (plus $1 for each book's postage and handling) to:

**First Teacher, Inc.
Box 29
60 Main St.
Bridgeport, CT. 06602**

OR CALL: 1-800-341-1522

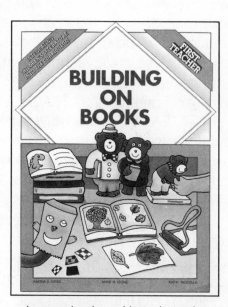

Q: WHERE CAN YOU FIND HUNDREDS OF CLASSROOM TESTED IDEAS *EACH MONTH* TO HELP YOUR CHILDREN LEARN AND GROW?

A: IN FIRST TEACHER

Each 16 page issue of FIRST TEACHER provides you with innovative projects to make each day an exciting new adventure. We give you ideas for toymaking, games and recipes to do with young children. We take you to the world of make believe with ideas for drama and creative movement. And experts recommend the very best books for young children in FIRST TEACHER.

FIRST TEACHER has a newspaper format, but it's something to read and save. Each issue has a topical theme, so each one adds a permanent resource of projects and ideas to your school or center.

FIRST TEACHER is written by experienced caregivers, daycare directors, and nursery teachers, so it's full of tested ideas to help you guide and motivate young children

FIRST TEACHER has been read and used by over 30,000 Early Childhood teachers. Here's what one of them, Racelle Mednikow, preschool teacher for 16 years, says:

"What a pleasure to be provided with well written, resourceful and usable ideas that can be interjected into our everyday curriculum and be of true value to each of our teachers!"

"Thank you so much for this delightful, informative newspaper."

Subscribe today! Don't miss another month of ideas, projects, and activities.
